Samuel H. Ford

The Great Pyramid of Egypt

The historic, geographic, scientific, prophetic, and eschatologic disclosures of the oldest and most gigantic of all the works of man

Samuel H. Ford

The Great Pyramid of Egypt

The historic, geographic, scientific, prophetic, and eschatologic disclosures of the oldest and most gigantic of all the works of man

ISBN/EAN: 9783337240103

Printed in Europe, USA, Canada, Australia, Japan

Cover: Foto ©ninafisch / pixelio.de

More available books at **www.hansebooks.com**

THE
GREAT PYRAMID OF EGYPT:

THE
HISTORIC, GEOGRAPHIC, SCIENTIFIC, PROPHETIC, AND ESCHATOLOGIC DISCLOSURES OF THE OLDEST AND MOST GIGANTIC OF ALL THE WORKS OF MAN.

BY

S. H. FORD, D.D., LL.D.,

Editor of "Ford's Christian Repository," Author of "Historic Milestones," "Battle of Freedom," Etc.

ST. LOUIS:
Published at Office of Ford's Christian Repository,
1882.

Entered according to Act of Congress, in the year 1882, by

S. H. FORD,

In the Office of the Librarian of Congress at Washington.

To my Wife,

Sallie Rochester Ford,

WHO HAS BEEN MY COMPANION THROUGH LONG YEARS OF
LITERARY LABOR, AND INTIMATELY ASSOCIATED
WITH ME IN ALL THE STUDIES OF
THE GREAT PYRAMID,

THIS WORK

IS AFFECTIONATELY INSCRIBED BY

THE AUTHOR.

PREFACE.

HAVING been for years a deeply interested student of all that pertains to the Great Pyramid of Gizeh—one of the *seven wonders* of the Ancients, and the only one of the seven that remains: having had my very soul lifted to a pure and lofty realm of thought, and beheld fresh light and beauty play over scientific facts hitherto dry or obscure,—my estimate of the human race exalted, the origin of that race glorified, and my whole range of mental vision widened and cheered by these studies—I have, by request from various respectable sources, and by the spontaneous expression of large audiences to whom I have lectured in different sections, penned these pages, mainly as an interpretation of Piazzi Smyth's great scientific work, with the hope and assured feeling that the same pleasure and benefit will result to the reader that the endeavor has given to the writer.

S. H. FORD.

ST. LOUIS, June, 1882.

The numerous works quoted in this volume, both scientific and historic —have been carefully consulted by the author. No labor or expense has been spared to reach original sources and recent discoveries.

PART I.

THE GEOGRAPHICAL AND SCIENTIFIC POSITION AND SHAPINGS OF THE GREAT PYRAMID

Chapter I.
Egypt's Place in History.................... 9

Chapter II.
Egypt's Future—The Pyramid and the North Pole—R. A. Proctor's Problem of the Pyramid—Whence this Wisdom?..... 15

Chapter III.
The Physical Aspects of the Great Pyramid—Its Materials—Its size and its Position............................. 31

Chapter IV.
The Measures of the Great Pyramid—Base, Side—The Days, Hours, Minutes and Seconds in our True Year............. 40

Chapter V.
The Sun's Distance from the Earth Symbolized in the Peculiar Shaping of the Pyramid 48

Chapter VI.
The Precessional Cycle—The Clock of the Universe Symbolized in the Diagonal Lines of the Pyramid.................. 56

Chapter VII.
The Squaring of the Circle—The Problem of Ages Solved in the Great Pyramid... 63

Chapter VIII.
What was the Great Pyramid Built for?.... 69

PART II.

THE HISTORIC AND PROPHETIC APOCALYPSE OF THE GREAT PYRAMID

Chapter I.
The Entrance Forced 81

Chapter II.
The Descending Passage—the Dragon Star—the Downward Drift............... 93

Chapter III.
Sacred Time Measures — From Babel to Sinai 101

Chapter IV.
From Egypt to Bethlehem................ 111

Chapter V.
The Grand Corridor and Gospel Era — The Disrupted Rock and the Resurrection of Jesus............................. 117

Chapter VI.
The Gospel Symbolism of the Grand Corridor—A Parable in Stone 133

Chapter VII.
The Historic Parables and Prophecies..... 142

Chapter VIII.
Eschatology—The Great Tribulation....... 154

Chapter IX.
The King's Chamber—The Stone Chest and the Ark of the Covenant—The Jubilee Year—Christ's Coming and Kingdom.. 162

Chapter X.
The Pyramid and the Pleiades 177

Chapter XI.
The Cap Stone and Corner Stone......... 183

PART III.

APPENDIX.

I.
Measurements........................... 189

II.
Have not the Measures given in this Work been Contradicted?................... 191

III.
Letter from the Astronomer Royal for Scotland.. 199

IV.
Did the Caphtorim Build the Great Pyramid?................................... 202

V.
Full Diagram and Indications............. 205

VI.
Dr. Phillip Schaff's Objection............ 206

PART I.

The Geographical and Scientific Position and Shapings of the Great Pyramid

)-20--An Altar to יהוה   In the midst of Egypt.

CHAPTER I.

EGYPT'S PLACE IN HISTORY.

EGYPT, to-day, is a miracle of fulfilled prophecy.

In the days of Abraham, it was a civilized and powerful kingdom. When God delivered Israel from centuries of cruel oppression, Egypt was the most powerful, as the most advanced, nation upon the earth. When Judea rose to her zenith under the glorious reign of Solomon, an alliance was made with Pharaoh as a material advantage, if not an honor, to the wide-spread and victorious people of Israel. Centuries before Troy fell or Greece rose to power, there stood Memphis, on the banks of the Nile, with her temples and palaces and granaries, while mighty Thebes sent down on the bosom of that deified river her tributes of art and wealth to the Queen City of the Pharaohs.

But the crimes of Egypt invoked the curse of heaven—crimes surpassing in their beastly enormity all that was gigantic in her material grandeur. The sacred oracle pronounced her punishment and her doom—black as night and as terrible as dark. "The burden of Egypt," broke forth the inspired Isaiah: "Behold, the Lord rideth upon a swift cloud, and shall come into Egypt: and the idols of Egypt shall be moved at His presence, and the heart of Egypt shall melt in the midst of it, and the spirit of Egypt shall fail in the midst thereof." * * * "And the Egyptians will I give over into the hand of a cruel lord; and a fierce king shall rule over them, saith the Lord of Hosts." * "For thus saith the Lord God: The sword of the king of Babylon shall come upon thee. By the swords of the mighty will I cause thy multitude to fall, the terrible of the nations, all of them: and they shall spoil the pomp of Egypt, and all the multitude thereof shall be destroyed." † "And when I shall put thee out, I will cover the heaven, and make the stars thereof dark; I will cover the sun with a cloud, and the moon shall not give her light. All the bright lights of heaven will I make dark over thee, and set darkness upon thy land, saith the Lord God." ‡

When these inspired men wrote, Egypt was in her ancient glory, renowned in arms and arts, and ruled by a despot who was adored and dreaded as a god. All things pointed to the perpetuity of his kingdom and the permanency of his throne. But upon the summit of

---

* Izaiah 19: 1, 4.
† Ezekiel 32: 11, 12.
‡ Ezekiel 32: 7, 8.

Egypt's greatness and Pharaoh's pride the finger of prophecy wrote: "Thus saith the Lord God; Behold, I am against Pharaoh, king of Egypt, the great dragon that lieth in the midst of his rivers, which hath said, My river is mine own, and I have made it for myself." *
His ruin is announced and Egypt is doomed as the basest of kingdoms.

History records the literal fulfillment of these predictions. We know that Cambyses defeated the Egyptian army and effectually broke the power of the Pharaohs at the battle of Pellusium in the year 527 before Christ. Psammenetus, the last native king, yielded to the arms of Cambyses, who strewed the land with the ruins of her ancient grandeur, and Persia ruled Egypt with a rod of iron through centuries.

Next came the winged leopard of Macedon. At the battle of the Granicus Alexander utterly defeated the proud Persian, and the world was at his feet. Egypt fell into his hands. He signalized her subjugation by founding Alexandria on the Mediterranean, at one of the mouths of the Nile. At his death Egypt fell to the lot of one of his generals, Ptolemy. The Greek ruled it for centuries. Greek was the language of the court and of philosophy. The Greek held all positions of honor and trust. The ancient Egyptian was treated as a foreigner in the land of his fathers, and Egypt became the meanest

---

* Ezekiel 29: 3.

of nations. The Grecian rule continued till the battle of Actium, thirty years before the Christian era. Cleopatra, the beautiful, licentious queen of Egypt, the last of the Greek rulers, became her own murderer rather than grace the triumph of Augustus Cæsar. Egypt then passed into the hands of new masters, and was made a province of the world-embracing empire. Varied were its fortunes and cruel its suffering during its subjugation to Rome. Zenobia, the queen of Palmyra, wrested it from the Romans in the year A. D. 270. It was soon retaken and the conqueress carried to Rome to follow, laden with chains, the triumphal chariot of Aurelian.

At the division of the Empire, Egypt fell to the Eastern Empire, and was governed by the lords of Constantinople. For twelve years it became the province of its old masters, the Persians. Then a native Copt governed it in the name of Heraclius, Emperor of Rome. In attempting to make himself independent of his master, he invoked the assistance of the Arabs, and Omar, the successor of the Prophet, easily made himself master of Egypt. Under his ferocious rule a still harder fate awaited Egypt. The fanaticism of Omar—the Sword of God, as he was called—impelled him to exult in the destruction of that library which had been the pride of the Ptolemies, and unrivalled in the ancient world. Christian places of worship were given to the flames; and Christian worshipers were forced beneath the uplifted scimeter to acknowledge Mahomet as the prophet of God. Conflagrations and massacres filled the cup of Egyptian misery to the very brim. Egypt was again given into the hands of a cruel lord, and a fierce king ruled over it. Constantine retook Alexandria, but was soon driven out by the ferocious courage of the Islams, and Egypt became an appendage of the Arabian Emperor, whose capital was Bagdad.

Various sects and dynasties in their struggles for supremacy soaked the soil with human blood. Under one of these successful rivals, Cairo (*El Kahireh*, the triumph of God,) was founded. Anarchy, bloodshed, rival and short-lived rulers, invasions, desolation, and battles formed the record of almost every year, culminating in 1010, A. D., when El Hakin ruled and raved like a demon. In addition to his monstrous cruelties, he made the people pay him divine honors. Slain by his slaves, desolating wars followed between Negroes and Saracens, and between both and Bagdad. Then came the Crusaders, followed by pestilence, while Saladin gave momentary quiet by his more powerful mastery. Darker and darker grew the night of Egypt. A line of slave-Sultans called Mamelukes, recruited by continued importations of Tartar captives, ruled Egypt with fierce cruelty and rapine for over two hundred years—under whose ignoble reign a condition of degradation and vileness was reached which the imagination cannot picture.

Egypt now passed into the hands of the Turks. In 1798 Napoleon invaded it. He defeated the Mamelukes and subjugated Egypt. But the French were expelled in 1801, and Egypt was restored to the Turks. Six years afterwards the Mamelukes were exterminated by a wholesale barbarous massacre. The Khedive of Egypt is still nominally subject to the Sultan of Constantinople, while Egypt in *fact* is controlled by England and France. And so, after this blood-stained history of night and oppression, Egypt, with her two millions of Arabs and Copts, is dominated by the Egyptian Turks, who number but ten thousand of her native population.

Such is the record of Egypt's dark story, in veritable accord with the prediction of the inspired seer:

"When the Egyptians shall fight every one against his brother,
And every one against his neighbor;
City against city, and kingdom against kingdom.
And the spirit of Egypt shall fail in the midst thereof
And I will destroy the counsel thereof;
And the Egyptians will I give over into the hand of a cruel lord;
And a fierce king shall rule over them,
Saith the Lord of Hosts—(Isa. 19: 2, 4.)
And it shall be the basest of kingdoms;
Neither shall it exalt itself any more above the nations."
—*Ezekiel: 29, 15.*

CHAPTER II.

EGYPT'S FUTURE.

THESE prophecies, uttered 650 or 750 years before the Christian era—when Egypt was ruled by her native Pharaohs, and rose in voluptuous splendor and power above the nations of the earth—have been fulfilled in all their black and fearful details.

And now let the closing, and as yet unfulfilled, portion of that same burden of Egypt be noted. A future day—a change of front—a new and glorious era—is in store for that land of darkness and oppression; a day when "Egypt shall cry unto the Lord, because of the oppressors, and He shall send them a Savior and a great one, and He shall deliver them. And the Lord shall be known in Egypt and the Egyptian shall know the Lord in that day."

This era has not yet dawned. Egypt is still without the knowledge of the true God. The crescent still rules its spiritual night. The oppressor still governs its ignorant and obscure people. But the fulfillment of the prediction of her future deliverance and renovation is as sure as the fulfillment of the prophecy of her past is patent. The latter is a matter of historic fact; the other is a matter of assured expectancy.

But before that day dawns, or at its very dawning, it is declared by the unerring oracle: "In that day shall there be an altar unto the Lord in the midst of the land of Egypt, and a pillar on the border thereof to the Lord. And it shall be for a sign and for a witness unto the Lord of Hosts in the land of Egypt." *

Now, there does stand in the very midst of the land of Egypt a mighty monument—the loftiest edifice ever reared by human hands; and this towering pillar is so situated that while in the midst it is on the border of the land of Egypt.

The accompanying outline map of Egypt will show that it is fan-shaped. Professor H. Mitchell, of the United States Survey, was sent by the Government in 1868 to report upon the progress of the Suez Canal. Struck with the peculiar formation of Egypt's northern coast, he sought for the central point of the successive curves. With the curvature of the northern coast on a good map before him, Prof. Mitchell searched with variations of direction and radius until he had got all the prominent coast points to be evenly swept by his arc; and then looking to see where his center was, found it upon the Great Pyramid, immediately deciding in his mind "that that monument stands in a more important physical relation than any other building ever erected by man."

---

* Isaiah 19: 19, 20.

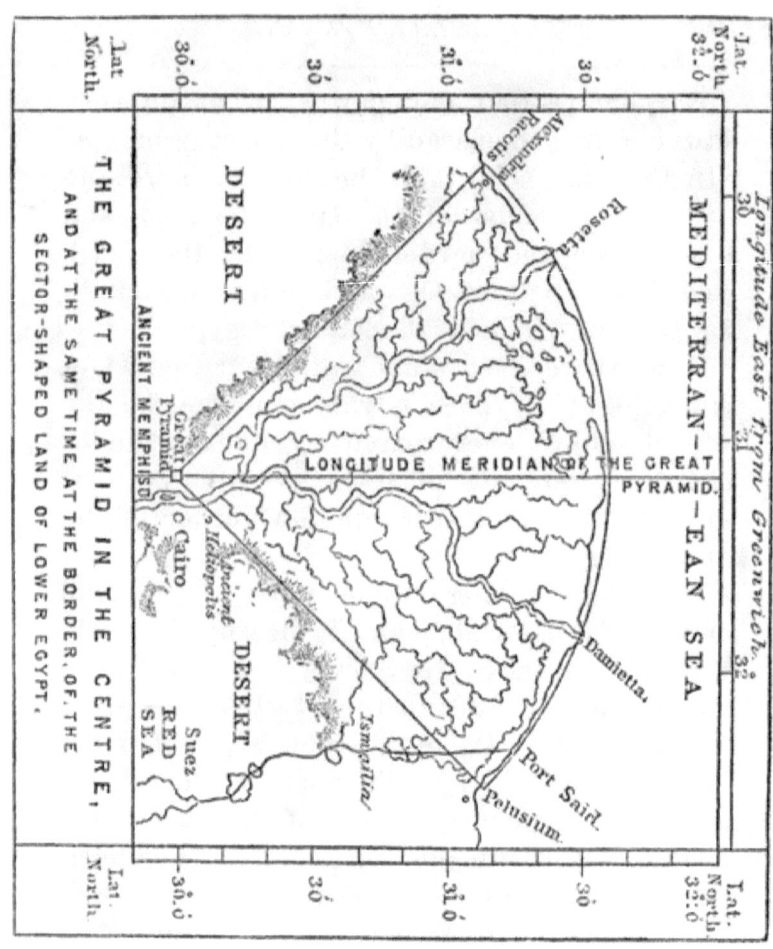

MAP OF EGYPT.

Led by no theory of the Pyramid, and with no reference, if, indeed, any recollection or knowledge of the prediction of a monumental pillar in the midst and on the border of Egypt, he found that this towering column stands in the midst of Lower Egypt, and yet on the border of its fan-shaped outline. Other smaller pyramids are there. But the one "close to the northern cliff of the Gizeh hill looks out with commanding gaze over the sectoral or fan-shaped land of Lower Egypt—from the land's very center of origin, or as from the handle of a fan outward to the far-off sea coast. All the other pyramids are away back on the table land south of the great one; so that they lose that grand view from the front or northern edge."

Egypt, as in no other land on earth, has a border-point for its center. At the center (and at the same time border point) rises this massive superstructure from a base of thirteen acres, and swelling in its symmetrical proportions to 484 feet high. Is this the predicted altar and pillar in the midst of the land of Egypt, and on the border thereof? What other spot in Egypt or on earth meets the requirement of the prediction? The prophecy points to the very spot on which the pyramid is built. And there stands the silent monitor—"a sign and a witness unto the Lord in the land of Egypt."

Commentators have usually passed over this remarkable passage with scarce a word of explanation. Some have given to it a mystic or figurative significance. But there is the literal statement: *It shall be for a sign and for a witness unto the Lord in the land of Egypt.* It has however, been recognized by recent eminent commentators as indicating a material altar or pillar. * Is there any example of a stone altar piled for such purpose?

Now, we read that the children of Reuben and the children of Gad and the half tribe of Manasseh, when they came to the borders of Jordan, "built THERE AN ALTAR BY JORDAN— A GREAT ALTAR TO SEE TO "—or to the view.

They were asked why they built this alongside of the altar of the Lord; they answered that they had built it *not for an altar of burnt offering nor for sacrifice,* "but for fear of this thing, saying, in time to come your children might speak unto our children, saying, What have ye to do with the Lord God of Israel?" "*That it may be for a witness between us, and you, and our generations after us, that we might do the service of the Lord.*"

And they called the altar '*Ed*'—*i. e.* witness —"for it shall be a witness between us that JEHOVAH HE IS GOD." †

Similar language is used by the prophet Isaiah in regard to the altar and pillar in the midst and yet on the borders of the land of Egypt.

---

* Jameson, Faucett and Brown, and others.
† Joshua 22.

It shall be for a sign and for a witness unto Jehovah in the land of Egypt.

Shrouded through centuries, it stood on this border land looking down on the rise and fall of empires, on the wreck of countless generations borne to oblivion on the tide of Time, unmoved amid the mutations which have leveled to the dust all cotemporaries. It has in these last days been unveiled, and stands uncovered as a monument for God. Like a witness long lost sight of and wrapt in silence, it has suddenly been brought into court to give forth its testimony—a witness to Jehovah in the Land of Egypt.

CHAPTER II.

THE PYRAMID AND THE NORTH POLE — R. A. PROCTOR'S PROBLEM OF THE PYRAMID — WHENCE THIS WISDOM?

"SOLDIERS of France," said Napoleon at the battle of the Pyramids, as the Turkish cavalry were thundering down like a simoon from the desert upon his front; "FORTY CENTURIES ARE LOOKING DOWN UPON YOU FROM THE SUMMIT OF THE PYRAMIDS." And from the summit of this lofty structure we can look down, or rather back, upon the builders of that wonder of the ages, and mark the design and the extent of their almost superhuman work.

Forty centuries—four thousand and sixty years—have passed since it was completed. Writings upon loose stones found in hollows in the building, as well as astronomical calculations hereafter to be described, prove these dates. What kind of men must they have been who projected and reared that immense pile? What could have been their object or design? Have the purposes for which they planned and built it ever been accomplished? Is it a message from the men who lived in the light of earth's early morning, before hereditary decline, idolatry, and savagery debauched the race—a message coming over the intervening blackness of ages to these days of enlightenment, assuring us that with all our discoveries, with all our attainments we have not reached the heights occupied by the progenitors of the race—that we have sprung from a glorious ancestry, and that we are not the offspring of the oyster or the descendants of baboons?

The Great Pyramid of Egypt, some ten miles from the Nile, stands on thirteen acres and a fraction of ground—equal to four of our city blocks, including streets and alleys. A rock hill has been leveled, and on this foundation, measured off with accuracy so as to meet the mathematical proportions of the building, a vast structure, with four sloping sides, has been raised to the height of nearly five hundred feet —the largest and the highest building ever reared by human hands.

At each corner of this thirteen-acre foundation, square holes were cut, called corner sockets. They were first uncovered by the engineers who accompanied Napoleon on his expedition into Egypt. The wear of centuries has defaced the corners of the Pyramid, but the socket holes tell exactly the original corners of the building. By means of these, not only have the base sides of the Pyramid been measured and their original length found, but it has been scientifically ascertained that they laid off the foundation due north, south, east and west, or, in other words, the builders of the Pyramid four thousand years ago *oriented* the work; that is, laid it off according to the four cardinal points of the compass, in accordance with the most refined principles of modern scientific astronomy.

It is not generally known that to orient a building, or to get the true north point, is one of the most difficult things in *practical* science. For, let it be observed that what we term Polaris, or the north star, is not the true north. There are a number of stars called *circumpolar*, which never pass below the horizon, but continually revolve around a fixed point in the heavens. Very near to this fixed point is the one we call the North, or Pole star. To the eye it seems stationary, but it also slowly revolves about this fixed point. Now, the difficulty in knowing the true north is to find the central point around which these *circumpolar* stars revolve—the centre of that circle around which the North star travels every twenty-four hours. How is this to be done? In addition to this, there is a real, or apparent movement of all the stars and galaxies in the universe. It is called the precessional cycle. By this the circumpolar stars change place, or fall back fifty seconds and a fraction every year. And from this it results that "the same star is not the Pole-star in different ages. In the course of thirteen thousand years a bright star, called Vega, which is now fifty-four degrees from the pole, will be less than five degrees, and will then be the Pole-star. *

How, then, with the movement of the Pole-star around a central point, and this change of places in the circumpolar stars, is the true north point to be ascertained?

Richard A. Proctor, the best known of living descriptive astronomers, wrote an article in the *Cotemporary Review* for September, 1879, in which he says: "I think that if there is one purpose among, probably, many which the builders of the Pyramids had in their thoughts which can be unmistakably inferred from the Pyramids themselves, independently of all tradition, it is the purpose of constructing edifices which should enable men to observe the heavenly bodies in some way not otherwise obtainable. If the orienting of the faces of the Pyramids had been effected in some such way as is used in the orienting of most of our cathedrals and churches—*i. e.*, in a manner quite sufficiently exact as tested by ordinary observation—it might reasonably enough be inferred, that having to erect square buildings for any purpose whatever, men were likely enough to set them four square to the cardinal points, and that therefore no stress whatever can be laid on this feature of the Pyramid's construction. *But when we find that the orient-*

---

* White's Theoretical and Descriptive Astronomy, p. 115.

ing of the Pyramid has been effected with extreme care, that in the CASE OF THE GREAT PYRAMID, *which is the typical edifice of this kind, the orienting bears well* THE CLOSEST ASTRONOMICAL SCRUTINY, *we cannot doubt that this feature indicates an astronomical purpose as surely as it indicates astronomical methods."*

Such is the acknowledgment of an oracle of modern astronomy. He admits the true orientation of the great Pyramid—" bearing the closest astronomical scrutiny." He acknowledges that this feature indicates the use of astronomical methods. What! were these *methods* known by the men of forty centuries ago? They are the boasted results of modern thought, improvement and research.

Professor Proctor essayed to account for this orientation of the Pyramid *a priori*, that is, by a system of guessing. He supposed that it was accomplished by the shadow method—just as a sun-dial marks off the shadow made by the rising sunbeam. But he acknowledged that in order to do this accurately, there must be a perfect level surface on which the sun-shadow falls. But how could a perfect level be obtained over thirteen acres? He *guessed* that water was forced from the Nile to cover the area, and by this means a level obtained. But. then, as the sides of the Pyramid are oriented —set due north, south, east and west, all the way up to the summit—the level must be found at every layer of rock all the way up. How to get rid of all this flood of water was a question. He *guessed* that the subterranean room was excavated to receive these numerous sheets of water, let off through what has been called the well running down into this room. But the writer of this showed that on the known effects of hydrostatic pressure the room and the whole foundation would have been shattered to fragments by this method.

But even if the orientation of the Pyramid was effected by the shadow method — which is next to impossible — it must be remembered that the first sun-dial of which there is any record, and evidently the first made in historic times, was erected in Rome three hundred and six years before Christ. * Eighteen hundred years before that discovery the Pyramid rose to its immense height strictly north and south, east and west — more accurately oriented than any known building of this day. Whence this wisdom ?

But Proctor gave up his scientific guesses, and acknowledges the superior wisdom of the Pyramid builders in these words:

"*The position of the base seems to prove beyond all possibility of question that the shadow method was not the method on which sole or chief reliance was placed, though this method must have been known to the builders of the Pyramid.*"

---

* George F. Chambers' Descriptive Astronomy, Oxford, 1867.

not know anything about the general arrangement of earth and sea surface over the globe, and that they were certainly ignorant of the existence of America and Australia, of New Zealand and Japan. This is all true.

They figured the earth in their hieroglyphics as a flat cake of bread. They could have no conception of a nether line or meridian on the opposite side of this globe-shaped earth. "Their astronomy," says Bunsen, "was strictly provincial, calculated only for the meridian of Egypt." And says Renan, "not a great poet, nor a great artist, not a *savant*, nor a philosopher, is to be found in all their history." What then? With no scrap of evidence that the imbruted slave-nation of the Pharaohs built the Pyramid; with no symbol or hieroglyphic of an idolatrous Egyptian character upon it; there it stands, in the center of the inhabitable lands of the earth, on the very spot sought for by the highest science as the starting point in reckoning distances around the earth, by the adoption of which all confusion in day countings would be avoided. There it stands, forcing on the mind the conviction, that a primitive, a lofty, an intellectual, a mighty race, with intuitive knowledge, or by divine aid and guidance, reared this *oldest and most gigantic of all human works* on a spot marking earth's center, as no other spot does, and pointing out the true north as even the Pole star fails to do.

CHAPTER IV.

THE MEASURES OF THE GREAT PYRAMID—BASE, SIDE — THE DAYS, HOURS, MINUTES AND SECONDS IN OUR TRUE YEAR.

THE thirteen acres which form the foundation of the Pyramid were laid off in a perfect square. Each side is a fraction less than 761 feet, or about the sixth of a mile. More accurately, according to the most recent measures obtained by scientific methods, each side is 9,130 inches. This is the original length of the base side as measured from the corner socket-holes, as dilapidations have abridged the length in the building itself by several feet.

These corner-holes or sockets were first uncovered by the engineers or *savans* who accompanied Napoleon into Egypt, in the year 1799. They published an account of their discoveries in a work entitled "*Description d'Antiquités.*" After digging down through the rubbish heaped up about the lower part of the building, "they recognized perfectly the esplanade upon which the Great Pyramid had been originally established; and discovered, happily, at the northeast angle, a large hollow socket worked in the rock, cut rectangularly, and uninjured, where the corner-stone had been placed; it is an irregular square which is 3 mètres (118 English inches) broad, in one direction, and 3.52 mètres (137.8 inches) in another." "They made the same research at the north-west angle, and there also discovered a hollow socket (*encastrement*) similar to the former. The two were on the same level. It was with much care and precaution that they measured the base side. They found it to be 233.747 mètres," or 763.62 British feet. *

These corner-stones were again uncovered by Col. Howard Vyse in 1837, and again, in 1865, by Acton and Inglis, of the British Ordnance Survey, in the presence of Smyth, the astronomer, and finally, in 1869, when the English Royal Engineer Surveyors returning from the Sinai Survey, were ordered to go to the Great Pyramid for the special object of measuring its base sides. The result announced by them was, that the length of a side from socket to socket was 9,130 British inches.

Without entering upon the variations in the different measurements by the French, by Col. Howard Vyse, by Acton and Inglis, this last result may be relied upon as the *mean* between

---

* *Description d'Antiquités*, Vol. II. The original French is quoted by Smyth in his "Inheritance in the Great Pyramid," p. 24.

all the others, as well as being obtained by the most recent and improved methods and instruments.

But these are British inches, and it is necessary to explain that this inch could not have been the unit of measure of the Great Pyramid. It leaves fractions in all the measurements, which an inch, a fine hair-breadth longer than our inch, will not leave. This longer one, by about one-thousandth part of an inch, is what is called the Pyramid inch. It is so visibly marked in the measurements of the Pyramid, that, as we proceed, it will be seen it must have been the unit of measure used by the architects of the building.

Now, each base side measures 9131 of those pyramid inches, and this length of each side was essential to the expression or solution of the grandest and most important problems in nature, viz.: the length of the true year, the precessional cycle, the quadrature of the circle, and the distance of the sun from the earth. To each of these problems, expressed or solved in the shapings of this vast structure, our attention will now be turned.

Our inch, hand-breadth, span, foot, cubit, and yard, or pace, have all the human form for a standard. The thumb is the standard of one inch; the hand-breadth of four inches; the span, eight inches; the foot, twelve; the elbow or arm, seventeen, and the step or pace, thirty-six inches. But as human feet and hands differ in size, these are not invariable as true standards of measure. Now, there is a unit of measure: an inch stamped upon the earth's polar axis, which is one-thousandth part, or a very fine hair-breadth longer than our common inch. That is to say, the distance through the earth from one pole to the other, called the polar axis, is, according to the British Ordnance Survey, five hundred millions, four hundred and twenty-eight thousand, two hundred and ninety-six of our inches. Beckett Dennison, in his Astronomy, gives five hundred millions five hundred thousand as the length of the polar axis, as the result of the most reliable modern calculations. Now this would make just five hundred millions of those inches which were the unit of measure in the plans of the Great Pyramid — an inch which is one thousandth part longer than the British inch. Then it is demonstrated that with this pyramid inch the earth's polar diameter measures, with no fractional remainder, five hundred millions of inches. From this it would appear that "God, who continually geometrizes," as Plato said, laid off earth's central line from pole to pole by the inch marked in the measures of the Pyramid. At least it is certain that the inch or unit of measure in the Pyramid — that which measures its various lines without fractional remainders and with corresponding adjustments—is the inch that measures the earth's polar diameter without a fractional remainder.

But more than this, it is found that twenty-five of these earth-measuring inches (or, as they are now called, pyramid inches) were the length of the sacred cubit of the Hebrews—the standard rule given by the Lord to Moses, by which to measure the Ark and the Tabernacle.

The length of the cubits of Babylon, Persia, and Egypt was some five inches less than the *sacred* cubit. We therefore read of the "iron bedstead of Og, king of Bashan," being "nine cubits the length thereof, and four cubits the breadth of it, after the cubit of a man." * Here is the distinction marked between the cubit of a man and the cubit which God gave.

In Ezekiel's vision of the Temple, we read:

"And these are the measures of the altar after the [sacred] cubits. The cubit is a [man's] cubit and a hand-breadth." And again, "Behold a wall on the outside of the house round about, and in the man's hand a measuring reed of six cubits, BY THE CUBIT AND A HAND-BREADTH." † Hence it is placed beyond question that the Lord's cubit differed from the "cubit of a man," the sacred cubit from the profane, and that this sacred cubit was a hand-breadth, or some four inches, longer than the Egyptian cubit, (nearly) 21 of our inches.

Two hundred years ago Sir Isaac Newton, in a dissertation on cubits, proved, (1) from

---

* Ezekiel 43 : 13. Chap. 40. 5.
† Deut. 3 : 11.

the Talmudist's proportion of the human body;
(2) from Josephus' description of the pillars of
the Temple; (3) from the length of a Jewish
sabbath day's journey; (5) by measure of the
steps in the inner court of the Temple; (6) from
the Chaldaic and Hebrew proportions to the
cubit of Memphis, and (7) from the statement
by Messennus as to the length of a supposed
copy of the sacred cubit of the Hebrews secretly
preserved amongst them—*that the Israelites had
a sacred cubit long before they went down into
Egypt.* He proved that this cubit was longer
by several inches than the Egyptian one, and
that the sacred cubit was treasured up by
Israel and employed for sacred purposes only.
The length of this cubit Newton showed to be
twenty-five and seven-hundreths of our inch,
with a possible error on one side or the other.
This approximate length of the sacred cubit
has been determined by more recent calculations to be exactly twenty-five and twenty-five
thousandths of our inch. This is, to a fraction,
the twenty-five inch cubit which is in several
ways stamped upon the Pyramid.

There is a deep sunken niche in one of the
interior rooms, soon to be described, which unmistakably marks this sacred cubit. It is not
in the central vertical line of the wall, but is
southward just the exact quantity of the sacred
cubit, 25.025 English inches, or 25 earth-measuring and pyramid inches. The deep niche was
evidently sunk there to mark off the twenty-

five inch sacred cubit—that is, *five times five* of those inches of which *five* hundred millions measure, without a remainder, the earth's polar axis.

Now going back to the accurately-measured length of each side of the Pyramid's base of 9131 inches, and dividing this number by the sacred cubit which is marked off on the wall of the queen's chamber, the result is:

$$9131 \div 25 = 365.242 +$$

Now the length of our tropical year is 365.242 + This in days and parts of a day is 365 days, 5 hours, 48 minutes and 49 seconds, with an impracticable fraction. This result agrees *minutely* with the symbolization of the Pyramid. The days, hours, minutes and seconds composing our solar year are stamped upon the stony leaves of this massive and mysterious book. The added lengths of the four sides of the base equal 36524.2 of those same pyramid inches, or at the rate of just one hundred for each day and part of a day of the year.

All this could not be mere accident. It is evident that the architects of the Pyramid knew the length of the year and laid off its 9131 inches of base-side length so that the days, hours, minutes and seconds which make up the true year should be plainly symbolized in the Pyramid's construction.

Now we know that the ancient nations—and even the Greeks in their palmiest days of knowledge — determined the length of the year by the moon. Twelve lunar months, making 354 days, made their year. This being found to be eleven days defective, eleven days had to be added in order to preserve the year in constant relative position to the seasons. The Egyptians, who divided their year into three seasons of four months each of thirty days, added five days to the end of the twelfth month. Not till the time of Cæsar was the solar year of 365 days 6 hours adopted by the Romans. But this solar year, to its minutest fraction, was known to the builders of the Pyramid two thousand years before the adoption of the Julian calendar.

Again may it be asked, *Whence this wisdom ?* Did it originate in the minds of the savage slaves of a barbarous despot? And if not, then what kind of men were the ancestors of our race?

CHAPTER V.

THE SUN'S DISTANCE FROM THE EARTH SYMBOLIZED IN THE PECULIAR SHAPING OF THE PYRAMID.

THE length of the solar year is dependent on the distance of the earth from the sun.

It is therefore a wonderful fact that in addition to marking off the foundation sides of the Pyramid so that it should number *exactly* as many sacred cubits as there are days in the year, the builders so shaped its four corners, from base to summit, that it would symbolize the earth's distance from the sun.

The Pyramid has that angle at the sides (to be noticed directly) which brings out the proportion of a diameter to the circle known as π. But it has another acuter angle at its *corners*. Thus for every *ten* units which the structure advances inward it rises *nine* of the same units sunward. To have a clear conception of this, let the reader imagine himself standing at one of the corners of the Pyramid and looking up to its top. The distance inward at each step at this *corner* will be, as a necessity, greater than the distance inward at the *sides* of the building. And the slope will be less steep all the way up to the top. Now this slope is an angle of

41° 59' 18.7", while the sides slope inward at an angle of 51° 51' 14.3". This latter angle was essential to the proportion of a diameter to the circumference of a circle; the other to this proportion of 10 inches inward to 9 sunward. And so this 10 by 9 proportion is stamped on the Pyramid's receding and ascending layers of solid rock as it was also on the casing stones which at first "*shingled*" it from pavement to apex.

This nine by ten shaping of the Pyramid proves that its architects understood—

Our System of Enumeration.

The very name of the Pyramid is said, by Chevalier Bunsen, to mean *Pyr*, "division"—like *peres*, "divided," as interpreted by Daniel—and *met*, "ten," that is, the division of ten. Ten and its division, five, are marked all over the shapings of the vast structure. The evidences are plain on the lines of the Great Pyramid that its architects knew the powers by this decimal system. And how wondrous that simple system is! If it is not divinely derived, it is the greatest achievement of the human intellect. Do we ever think of the completeness of this system of tens—how changing the position of a figure increases it ten-fold—how the 3 becomes 30, and then 300, and then 3000, and on to millions and trillions simply by putting the 3 farther along in the line of figures? Logarithms in their almost infinite calculations are based on this simple element. Was ever anything invented by man more wonderful than this? Can anything he can do or imagine surpass it? Yet this was known to the builders of the Pyramid, for there it is stamped upon its shapings.

Nine, the climax and the amount of our system of numeration, is everywhere seen marked on the Pyramid. There are four sides and five corners (including the head corner), making nine. There are nine thousand and a ninth inches in each of its base sides. There are four times nine great granite stones spanning its grand gallery, while this nine by ten shaping is a characteristic of the work.

Now how wonderful these nine digits! They meet all the wants of science in its vast calculations. They meet all the needs of commerce. It is impossible to conceive of any improvement or addition to those nine simple digits, which must have been conceived and used before letters, or our so-called Arabian characters, were used to express them.

"The idea of number," says Greenleaf, "is the latest and most difficult to form. Before the mind can arrive at such an abstract conception it must be familiar with that process of classification by which we successively ascend from individuals to species, from species to genera, from genera to orders. The savage is lost in his attempts at numeration, and significantly expresses his inability to proceed by holding up his expanded fingers or pointing to the hairs of his head." And how could savage or semi-savage, or even highly educated men, unaided, originate the system which meets every requirement of almost infinite calculation, and the improvement of which cannot even be imagined?

Did the reader ever ponder the peculiar powers of this number nine? One only can be mentioned in passing. In all its multiplication nine will be found in the result. Twice 9 are 18, and the 8 and 1 are 9. Three times 9 are 27, and the 2 and 7 are 9. It is so up to 9 times 20 =180, the 1 and 8 are 9. Then commencing at 21 the sum is 189, two 9s. Going on in this series of multiplying by a system, 9 is found in the added results without a remainder through all its multiplication. This may also be classed with accidents; but to any honest-thinking mind there is thorough design, well-planned system in it. Who originated it? It is traced as far back as primitive man, whose life was nine hundred years. It is stamped on the Pyramid, the *oldest* as it is the most gigantic of human work. Were these primitive men familiar with "the *idea* of number—the latest and most difficult to form?" Or was this *idea* of number God-given and beyond the powers of human invention?

But leaving this, we turn again to the fact stamped on the diagonal shapings of the Pyramid. Its corners recede inward ten units for every nine which it rises sunward. Now this nine by ten indicates 10^9; that is, 10 raised to its ninth power, or one thousand millions, and this result, multiplied by the Pyramid's height and reduced to English miles, gives the distance of the sun from the earth.

Mr. Petrie having found that the circle typified by the base symbolized a year, or the earth's annual revolution round the sun, concluded that the sun's distance was represented by the vertical height, and in proportion to 10^9, or 1,000,000,000. Mr. Petrie at once took the 10^9, or ten raised to its ninth power, one thousand millions, and multiplied this by the height of the Pyramid, 5,818.+ English inches, making 5,818,000,000,000 inches, and reduced this to English miles. The result was 91,840,000.

But the then mathematically established distance of the sun from the earth was ninety-five millions and over. The calculations of the Pyramid's 10^9 came short by over three millions of the real sun's distance, as settled by the highest authorities in astronomy. Mr. Petrie, therefore, threw away his papers and calculations, and would have thought no more of them, but that while occupied in his professional chemical engineering, he read in the scientific journals, that this number as the sun's distance, undisputed so long, was erroneous.

Observations had been made, and results collected from both hemispheres, and the newly computed sun-distance given to the world. One group of astronomers of several nations declared the true mean sun-distance to be about ninety-one and a half millions of miles.

Another group of the same, and of other nations, announced it to be from ninety-two and a half to ninety-three millions of miles. Such was the intensity of interest felt in this discussion that a duel of swords was expected and prepared for between two of the highest living authorities in astronomy — M. Le Verrier, and M. DeLaunay. In the midst of this disputation, Mr. Petrie returned to the calculations he had made years before from the ten by nine shaping of the Pyramid, and showed that the result from them was exactly the mean between the figures insisted on by the contending astronomers—and that this result, stamped on the Pyramid, is in itself, and in all its grand simplicity and antiquity, a simple representation of all the laborious and expensive efforts to find the true sun-distance.

The expensive arrangements made by different nations to observe the transit of Venus in 1874, and the years of untiring calculations which have followed those observations, show how difficult is the task to find the true distance of the sun. The Greeks supposed it was ten miles. They increased this to ten thousand. After long centuries, advanced science again increased this to two millions and a half. Then Kepler showed it to be thirty-six millions. Abbé LaCaille, of France, by means of transequatorial observations, declared it to be seventy-eight millions. The leaders of mathematical astronomy at the beginning of this century, after years of patience and vast calculations, announced it to be a little over ninety-five millions. Then came the world-united effort in 1874, to ascertain the true figures. Iron ships, electric telegraphs, exquisite telescopes, photographic machines of enormous power, chemicals of wondrous nicety as well as of deadly subtlety, refined regulator clocks, and still more refined chronographs, transit instruments, equatorial spectroscopes, polariscopes, altitude-azimuth circles, with every modern invention that could aid,—were made tributary to the grand effort to find the distance of the sun from the earth. But men who had studied the Pyramid declared the result was there, stamped on its shapings four thousand years ago.

The expensive national expeditions of 1874, to observe the transit of Venus claimed to be successful. Years have passed and some of the results have been given to the public :

First—The Astronomer Royal of Greenwich was called on to report to the English Parliament the new sun-distance. He reported it as ninety-three millions and some hundreds of thousands of miles.

This report and its accompanying papers were reviewed by the Royal Astronomer, at the Cape of Good Hope, and found erroneous—the true result being ninety-one millions and some hundred thousands of miles.

The Greenwich astronomers then revised

their report and reduced the result to nearly the same figures indicated in South Africa.

Second—A notable member in the French Academy, M. Puiseux, computed some of the observations of *two* of the French Venus-Transit Stations, viz.: Pekin and the Island of St. Paul, in the Indian Ocean. From these he deduced the sun distance to be 91,840,271 miles.

Now, the 10^9 of the Pyramid's shape—that is 5,818+ inches, its height, multiplied by one thousand millions, brings 91,840, only 270 miles less than the French savant's result, and about the same as the English estimate which Prof. R. A. Proctor pronounces a satisfactory one.

Is not this wonderful? When M. Puiseux's computations were announced in the Paris scientific journal called *Les Mondes,* Chanoine Moigno, the editor, accompanied it with the exclamation: *La Grande Pyramide a vaincu!*—THE GREAT PYRAMID HAS CONQUERED!

It has stamped upon it in symbols which no change in language can affect, this knowledge which, with all assistance of governments and all the aid of astronomical and mathematical instruments, the men of this day cannot attain to. How did the architects of the Pyramid attain to it? Could men in that early day, when they were comparatively few, and confined to a limited portion of earth's surface, grasp and solve these sublime problems? Yet there is the solution in that "oldest and most gigantic of human works."

Whence this wisdom?

CHAPTER VI.

THE PRECESSIONAL CYCLE—THE CLOCK OF THE UNIVERSE SYMBOLIZED IN THE DIAGONAL LINES OF THE PYRAMID.

WE have seen that the sacred cubit of twenty-five inches is contained 36524 times in the base side length of the Pyramid—that is, there are to a fraction the number of cubits in each side that there are days, hours, minutes and seconds in our true year. But there is a grander movement than this observable in the heavens. It is the real or apparent march of all worlds and star-galaxies along a circuit of unmeasured millions of miles. It takes each star nearly twenty-six millions of years to complete this circuit. This stellar round has been very properly termed the grand chronological dial or clock of the universe. It is the PRECESSIONAL CYCLE. "The appearance is as though the equinox goes forth to meet the sun; and hence the phenomenon is called the precession of the equinoxes. The scientific expression of this fact is, by saying that the equinoxes retrograde on the ecliptic until the line of the equinoxes makes a complete revolution from east to west." *

---

* Olmstead's "Astronomy," p. 104.

But these scientific terms are but feebly apprehended even by educated people. We know what it is for one event to precede another. We know that equinox means equal nights, or the time when the days and nights are equal. We know that this occurs on the 21st of March or on the 22d of September—called respectively the vernal and autumnal equinox. A simple illustration will make it plain to all:

Suppose we go to a selected spot, say the 22d of September, 1881, at 12 o'clock at night by exact sun-time, and notice a star immediately over our heads. We mark the spot where we stand, and observe the star (not a planet, of course,) so that we shall recognize it again. Suppose we return to that identical spot one year from that date—22d September, 1882, at the same moment by exact sun-time, and look up for that same star. It is not where it was one year before. It has moved eastward (50.1″) fifty and one-tenth seconds of a degree. Suppose we come to the same spot at the same instant the next year, it will have moved on an additional fifty seconds and one-tenth. The following year it will have moved another fifty seconds, and still *on, on,* every year fifty seconds and a fraction, until it has passed down the horizon and shines upon those on the opposite side of the globe at that instant of the 22d of September. And still it will move on in its steady time-beat, fifty seconds and a fraction every year, until it has passed along the whole circle of the heavens and returns to that same spot where it was seen above our heads the 22d of September, 1881. But twenty-five thousand six hundred and twenty-seven years have elapsed during that *Grand Cycle*. It takes those centuries for each star and galaxy to complete that stellar round in which all alike are moving to a wondrous measure. This is the precessional cycle—or precession of the equinoxes. It is the clock of eternity that beats years as ours beats minutes. *

By this celestial chronometer the time can be told when any star shines on a given spot and when it will shine there again.

This real or apparent movement of the stars, of 50".1 seconds of a degree, or 22 minutes 21 seconds of time, makes the whole length of the stellar round 25,827 years, according to the most recent and careful calculations. †

---

* LaGrange's "Astronomy."

† The difficulty of reckoning the time of this cycle will appear by noticing the following attempts to state the length of this period :

By Tycho Brahe	25,816 years
Cassini	24,800 "
Ricciolus	25,920 "
Bradley	25,740 "
La Place	25,816 "
Bessel	25,868 "
Herschel	25,868 "
Newcomb	25,800 "
White	25,817 "

This last quoted author is the authority in most of our

This peculiar celestial cycle, the grand chronological dial in fact of the Great Pyramid, is defined by the length of the two diagonals of the base. These two lines, from the opposite corners, lay out the whole portion of the structure. They are the two longest lines. Their added lengths are 25827 pyramid inches, equal to the mean result of all the varying calculations of the length in years of the precessional cycle.

Farther still this grand time cycle is memorialized in the upper and principal room in the Pyramid. The floor of this room is 1702 inches above the foundation. It has been shown by Professor Hamilton L. Smith, of Hobart College, New York, that the circuit of the Pyramid at the level of this room equals 25,827 pyramid inches—the length in years of the great precessional cycle. And Proctor has found the same symbolism, or as he calls it "coincidence, in the outside cubits when taken instead of inches."

These facts in regard to the precessional cycle make it (as *in fact* it is) the grand chronological dial of the Great Pyramid. By it Sir

---

universities and his work is used as a text book. Recent calculations make the length of the precessional period nearer to the figures he gives than to those given by Bessell. This difference grows out of the different measure of the annual precession. White makes it 51.2"; Herschell 51.1".

John Herschel told when a star looked down the descending passage of the Pyramid, thus identifying the time of its erection. By this greatest of time cycles, it is also found, as we shall see farther on, that the Pleiades were on the meridian at midnight, in Egypt, the year the Pyramid was completed. So that its summit pointed like an index finger to that central cluster around which all the starry hosts move. It will be seen from all this that those supposed shepherd kings who built the mighty structure in the very center of earth's habitable lands and on the border and yet in the midst of the land of Egypt, knew this movement of the stars, and were able to calculate, with an exactness that modern science has not reached, the *time of the precessional cycle—25,827 of our years.*

Whence this wisdom? Did these primitive men grasp at one bound this vast problem which the last three hundred years of patient research by the greatest of minds with all modern aid, have only partially solved? Were these "keepers of flocks" on the borders of the Lybian desert able to simplify those vast calculations in regard to the sun's distance and the precessional cycle, and stamp the results in readable symbols on that *oldest and most gigantic of all human works?* Few in this day of enlightenment can even follow out these calculations. Though they are taught in our school books, illustrated by engravings, explained in popular lectures, and made comparatively easy by telescopes and instruments of wonderful invention, yet how few can comprehend or even follow their methods, or form a clear conception of the grand facts! How then could the men of forty centuries ago have known them and embodied them in this memorial pile? Either there is proof of supernatural knowledge granted to the architects, or else those men, in an age of absolute scientific ignorance, possessed astronomical knowledge surpassing that attained to in this boasted nineteenth century.

And just as the true sun-distance is, by the very latest results of years and years of calculation, found to be that symbolized in the Pyramid's shapings, so the more recent calculations of the precession of the equinoxes, center upon the period marked by the added diagonal lines of the Pyramid—25,827 years. Again we ask, WHENCE THIS WISDOM?

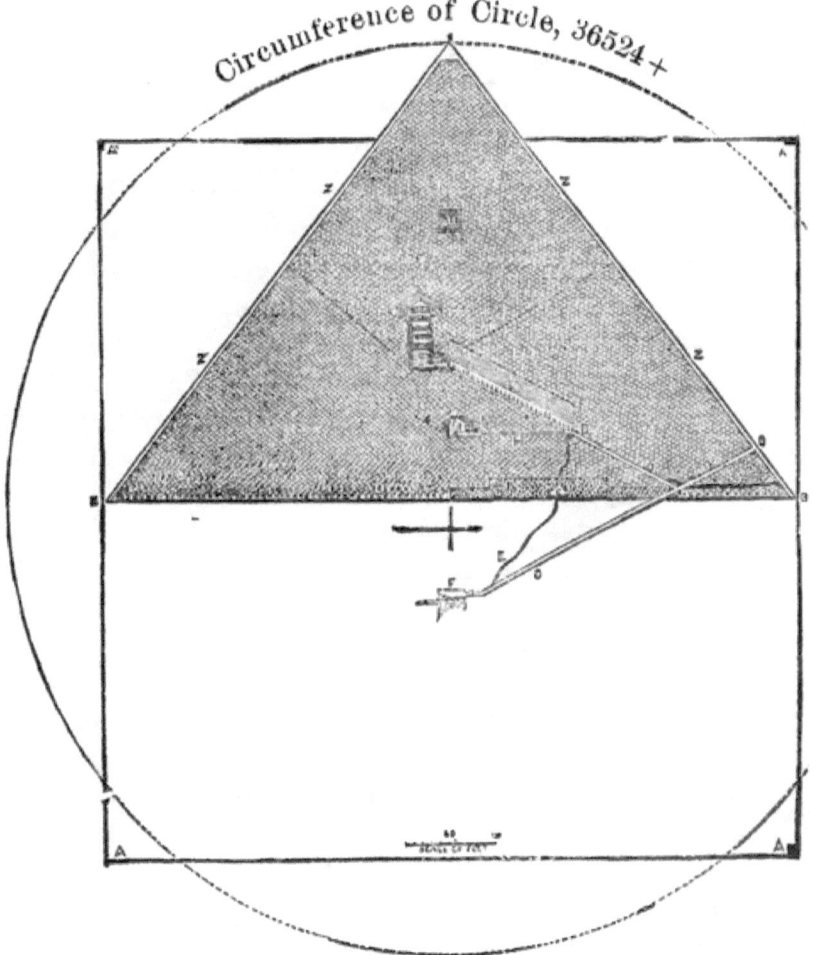

CHAPTER VI.

THE SQUARING OF THE CIRCLE—THE PROBLEM OF AGES SOLVED IN THE GREAT PYRAMID.

"THE quadrature of the circle," as it is called, "consists in finding a square equal in surface to a circle the radius of which is known."* The solution of this problem has interested mathematicians from the days of Archimedes to the present hour. And quite right that it should. It is the basis alike of practical mathematics and high astronomy. In Dr. Olinthus Gregory's great work entitled "Mathematics for Practical Men," the uses of this problem are given in fifty-four different forms, showing its value in mechanical constructions. Years since, the Royal Society of London, and also the Academy of Science of Paris, offered a prize to any one who would *fully* solve this problem, and the fractional answer was run out to the two hundredth decimal place, still leaving it with an infinitesimal plus.

Now the Pyramid is just such a height, consequent on a particular angle of slope, that this height is the radius of a circle equal to the four sides of the base—thus practically solving the *problem of the ages.*

---

* Davies' Legendre, Book 5, Prop. 16.

In other words, the builders of the Pyramid laid off the foundation in the form of a "*square equivalent in surface to a circle the radius of which was known.*" * This radius was the vertical height of the Pyramid. The radius of such a circle *must be known*. The Pyramid had consequently to be built at such an angle of inclination that the height should be this *known* radius. " To square the circle (says Legendre) is to find the circumference where the radius is given, and for effecting this, it is enough to know the ratio of the diameter to the circumference." Now, these progenitors of the race planned a building of such peculiar shape and size that its height should be the radius of a circle equal exactly to the perimeter of the base. Hence, they must have known, when they laid off the foundation, what must be the surface of a square to be equal to such a circle as they had in mind. They had then to know what the *diameter* of such equal circle would be. They had then to plan the slope of the sides so as to make the height just half the diameter of this equal circle. All this must have been known before a stone was laid.

Whence the knowledge? Is it possible they possessed it?

Now it has been found (first by John Taylor,

---

* I use the words of Davies' Legendre in defining the quadrature of a circle to show how completely the Pyramid meets that definition.

of London, 1855,) that both in the receding courses of stones which form steps at the sides of the Pyramid, and also in the casing stones which originally fitted into these layers or steps, the angle of slope is 51° 51'. This angle of slope from the base upwards gives such a height to the structure as must necessarily result from this angle of slope. It is easy, therefore, (by finding where these angles of incline would meet each other) to calculate what was the original height of the structure. It has been demonstrated to have been originally 5813 pyramid inches.

Now this height was the *known radius*. What proportion does it bear to a circle? *This is the problem of the ages.* Can we believe that it was practically worked out and memorialized on the borders of the Lybian Desert forty centuries ago?

The original height of the Pyramid was 5813 inches. This was the known radius. Twice that number, 11626, was the diameter of a circle equivalent to the four sides of the base. The question to be solved by the architects of the Pyramid was this, *What ratio does this diameter bear to the square formed by the four sides of the base?*

Well, the four sides of the base, each one 9131+ inches, make 36524+ inches.

The diameter of the desired circle (twice the vertical height of the Pyramid) $5813 \times 2 = 11626$.

Now, then, to ascertain what proportion this

diameter has to the four sides the one is divided by the other, and the almost magical number is the result: 3.14159+.

Then, for all practical purposes, the problem is solved. The proportion of a diameter to a circle, and the square equal to a circle, were expressed in the height and four sides of the Pyramid in language which can never change or die while earth lasts or men live.

The architects of the Pyramid must have known these proportions before they planned the work. They must have determined the height of the structure and the angle of slope to a minute fraction so as to bring out the exact height. They must have known that this pre-determined height would be the length of a radius which would draw a circle whose circumference would be equivalent to a square of certain dimensions. These dimensions of the square were decided on 36524. Then what must the height be? This must be exactly 5813 inches to describe a circumference equal to four times the length of a side of the base. What angle of slope is necessary to this height? It is found to be of necessity, as a geometrical problem, 51°, 51' and 43.3". All these calculations, requiring the highest culture and profound thought, are worked out in the base side, the height, and the angles of the Great Pyramid. But all this could not have been done unless these men knew the π proportion—knew the 3.14159 ratio of a diameter to a circle. It is *certain* that these primitive men knew this mathematical proportion in a way few know it in these days of general enlightenment. They knew them and worked them out in this "*oldest and most gigantic of human work.*" They solved the most important and most difficult of problems, and impressed and expressed it on that lofty pile of massive rock which no change of language can affect, but which can be seen and read by all men of every age and tongue. *Whence this wisdom ?*

But this is not the only expressed solution of this quadrature of the circle in the plan of the Pyramid.

It was discovered by Capt. Tracy of the British Navy in 1873 that the pyramid inches in what is termed the King's Chamber (the principal room in the building) stand for cubits outside the Pyramid. From this the following results were deduced by eminent professional mathematicians : *

The length of the King's Chamber is 412,122 inches; take this as the side of a square, find its perimeter, and throw that into a circular shape. The radius of such a circle will be found to be the height of the Pyramid in cubits, viz : 232,520, thus expressing in another way the remarkable fact that the Pyramid's height is the radius of a

---

* Capt. William Petrie, Civil Engineer; Capt. Tracy, Royal Navy ; Prof. Hamilton Fish, Hobart College, N. Y.; H. B. Wrey, Tawstock, England.

circle which is equal to the sum of the four sides of the base.

This same feature is symbolized in another form by the length of this same King's Chamber, so that this problem of squaring the circle governs the whole design and shapings of the mighty structure.

Now, let any one calmly reflect on these disclosures and ask, Could it be that this knowledge belonged to men just emerging from savagery? Indeed it *may* be fairly asked, Could such knowledge, such profound thought, such mental grasp, such principles underlying astronomy and mechanical arts, have been possessed by men however strong and mighty, of that primitive age, unless communicated by eternal wisdom imparted to the first man and handed down along the line of those patriarchs of the race, whose lives numbered centuries? Any rational conclusion proves that the Biblical account of man's origin, and God's intercourse with him, is true.

CHAPTER VIII.

WHAT WAS THE GREAT PYRAMID BUILT FOR?

THE question may now be asked, For what object was the Pyramid built?

Various theories and traditions have been and still are advanced in answer to this question.

Josephus, the Jewish historian, relates as an historical verity that "Seth and his descendants were the inventors of that peculiar wisdom which is concerned with the heavenly bodies and their order," "and that their knowledge might not be lost they made two pillars, the one of brick the other of stone, to preserve their discoveries," adding, "*Now* this (pillar of stone) remains to this day in the land of Siriad (Egypt.)"*

The Arabians had a tradition very similar to the foregoing in a manuscript written by one *Aou Balkhi*, (preserved in the Bodlean Library in England and translated by Dr. Springer). The Arabian author says: "The wise men previous to the flood, foreseeing an impending judgment from heaven, either by a submersion or by fire, which would destroy every

---

* Jewish Antiquities.

living thing, built on the tops of the mountains in upper Egypt many pyramids of stone in order to have some refuge against the impending calamity. Two of those buildings exceeded the rest in height, being four hundred cubits high and as many broad and long. They were built of large blocks of stone, and were so well put together that the joints were scarcely perceptible. And upon the exterior of the building every charm and wonder of physics (natural science) was inscribed."

To this another Arab writer adds, "Likewise the positions of the stars and their circles, together with the history and chronicles of times past, of that which is to come, and of every future event."

Another eminent Arabian author, cotemporary with the author of the "Arabian Nights," named Ibn Abd Alkokm, gave out what he claimed to be a translation from an old Egyptian papyrus, that "*Shedded Ben Ad*, the great antediluvian king of the earth, built the Great Pyramid, and lodged within it divers celestial spheres and stars and what they severally operate in their aspects; and the perfumes which are to be used in them, and the books which treat of these matters," together with "the mysteries of science, astronomy, geometry and physic." *

---

* Quoted by P. Smyth.

Another of these Arabian romancers says, "It was constructed by Enoch to preserve the arts and sciences and other intelligence during the flood."

Of course no reliance can be placed in these Arabian writings. "The only fact," says Col. Howard Vyse, "which seems to be established by these Eastern writers is the opening of the Great Pyramid by Al Mamoun in the ninth century."

Some have thought that they were built as barricades against the sands of the desert sweeping over the low lands of Egypt, though a wall would have at once suggested itself for such a purpose.

The more general theory, both anciently and at present, is that the Pyramids were built for royal tombs, the Great Pyramid for King Chufa —called Cheops.

This was the name of the king supposed to have reigned over Egypt when the Great Pyramid was built. But Sir Gardiner Wilkinson, one of the highest authorities in Egyptology, says in his Guide Book to Egypt, "It may be doubted whether the body of the king was deposited in the sarcophagus;" while M. St. John does not consider the stone chest or coffer found in what is called the King's Chamber a sarcophagus at all, and holds that the building was never meant for a tomb. The idea of the Great Pyramid having been erected as a tomb for Cheops grew out of a misunderstanding of the language of Herodotus.

This charming narrator visited Egypt about 445 B. C. He made personal examination of the outside of the Pyramid, and then wrote down the statement of the Egyptian priest given to him through an interpreter. It is as follows:

"Now they told me that to the reign of Rhampsinitus there was a perfect distribution of justice, and that all Egypt was in a high state of prosperity; but that after him Cheops, coming to reign over them, plunged into every kind of wickedness; for that, having shut up all the temples, he first of all forbade them to offer sacrifice, and afterward he ordered all the Egyptians to work for himself; some, accordingly were appointed to draw stones from the quarries in the Arabian mountains down to the Nile, others he ordered to receive the stones when transported in vessels across the river, and to drag them to the mountain called the Libyan ; and they worked to the number of a hundred thousand men at a time, each party during three months. The time during which the people were thus harassed by toil lasted ten years on the road which they constructed, along which they drew the stones, a work, in my opinion, not much less than the pyramid ; for its length is five stades, and its width ten orgyæ, and its height where it is the highest, eight orgyæ; and it is of polished stone, with figures carved on it: on this road, then, ten years were expended, and in forming the subterraneous apartments on the hill, on which the Pyramids stand, which he had made as a burial vault for himself, in an island, formed by draining a canal from the Nile. Twenty years were spent in erecting the Pyramid itself: of this, which is square, each face is eight plethra, and the height is the same ; it is composed of polished stones, and jointed with the greatest exactness : none of the stones are less than thirty feet." *

That Herodotus was imposed upon by this priest, or misled by the interpreter, is certain, as there are no stones in the building measuring that length.

But that Chufa (or Cheops) was not buried in the Pyramid, even according to the priest's statement to Herodotus, is evident from the words "*a burial vault for himself in an island* formed by draining a canal from the Nile." Just such an island or locality built for a tomb, and with precisely the required hydraulic conditions, has recently been discovered one thousand feet from the Great Pyramid.

"The structure there found, and still to be seen, descended into, and measured, though much defiled by the 26th and later Dynasties of ancient Egypt in its decline,—is a colossally large and deep burial pit, on the square and level bottom of which rests an antique, rude

---

* Herodotus, B. 11, p 144-5, Carey's Translation.

sarcophagus of very gigantic proportions. But deep as is the pit containing it, it is surrounded by a grand rectangular trench which goes down deeper still, cut clearly in solid lime-stone rock the whole of the way down; and to such a depth does it reach at last as to descend below the level of the adjacent waters of the Nile at inundation time. Then, as the waters of that river necessarily percolate the hygroscopic rock of the hill up to their own level, the lower depths of the trench are filled with Nile water, and the grand old sarcophagus of the interior pit does then rest in a manner on an island surrounded by the waters of the Nile, exactly as Herodotus described;—and it is the only known tomb on the Jeezeh hill which is gifted with that peculiarity or privilege." *

This explanation of the words of Herodotus in regard to the place in which King Cheops was buried, together with the fact that the stone chest was found lidless in a room not closed up, and in which no mummy was ever found, has led men who have given their lives to the study of Egyptian history and monuments, to abandon the theory of the Pyramid being built for a tomb. M. Jomard, in his celebrated "*Description de l'Egypte*," after having studied all the features and aspects, with all the forms of old tombs and pyramids before him, wrote concern-

---

* See Piazzi Smyth's "Great Pyramid," p. 130.

ing this great one, "Everything is mysterious. I repeat it, in the construction and distribution of this monument, with its passages—oblique, horizontal, sharply bent, and of such different dimensions. We are not at all enlightened either upon the origin or the employment, the utility, or any motive whatever for the Grand Gallery and various passages."

There are no evidences that it was built for a tomb. There are no evidences worth naming that any one was ever buried in it. There are evidences that Cheops was buried as Herodotus describes, in an artificial island circled by the waters of the Nile.* For what then was the Great Pyramid built?

A popular encyclopedia published by Messrs. Appleton & Co. states in a somewhat confused way that a mummy was found in the Great Pyramid. There is not a shred of proof of this. Col. Vyse found a mummy in the third pyramid—in the underground chamber—but nothing of the kind was found in the Great Pyramid of Gizeh.

"Be this as it may," says Mr. Proctor, "it is certain that the pyramids were constructed for astronomical observation." And yet only when it was half finished, as this astronomer acknowledges, could it be of any avail for astronomical observation.

---

* *Contemporary Review*, Sept., 1879.

It was not a temple of worship. The massive pile is solid—except those passages leading to two small rooms, and these passages were blocked up seemingly for a design then far in the future.

It was the product of a civilization which the skeptic Renan admits had no infancy. It was built in a land which, this same skeptic admits, "never had a great poet, artist, *savant* or philosopher"—a land whose astronomy, says Brugsch Bey,* "was based on empiricism, not on that mathematical science which calculates the movements of the stars." And yet there it stands, the mighty proof of the highest astronomical and mathematical knowledge to which mankind has ever attained.

What was it built for, and who were its builders?

We shall be better prepared to answer after we have explored its inner passages.

---

* History of Egypt, vol. 1, p. 181.

THE LINK THAT BINDS.

"Dwelling like greatest things alone,
Nearest to Heaven of earthly buildings, thou
Dost lift thine ancient brow
In all the grandeur of immortal stone,
And, like the Centuries' beacon, stand,
Up-springing as a tongue of fire
To light the course of Time through Egypt's mystic land.

'Tis not for poets to inquire
Why thou wast built and *When?*
Whether, in monumental state,
So great thyself to tomb the great
Beyond their fellow-men?
Or dost thou, in thy bodily magnitude,
Not uninformed nor rude,
Declare the abstract ties which Science finds,
Seen by the light of *geometric* minds,
On fixed proportions, each allied to each?
Or dost thou still, in inferential speech,
Reveal unto mankind the *girth*
Of the vastly rounded earth ;
And to the busy human race
Bequeath a rule, to guide the range
Of all the minor measurements of Space,
Which Traffic gets, and gives, in endless interchange.

Enduring pile! Thou art the link that binds
The memory of reflective minds—
Vast mass of monumental rock sublime,
That to the present Age dost join the Youth of Time."

PART II.

THE HISTORIC AND PROPHETIC APOCALYPSE OF THE GREAT PYRAMID.

CHAPTER I.

THE ENTRANCE FORCED.

AND there stood the gigantic pile with unrecorded date, looking down upon the ruins of all contemporary monuments, steadfast upon its rocky hill—itself a mountain of stone, with all its avenues closed—the wonder and the mystery of the ages.

Abraham had gazed upon it in all its pristine glory. It was known to the patriarchs and to the children of Israel. Centuries swept by it. The storms of ages beat against it, and mighty armies battled for universal empire about its base. Herodotus, the first to write human history, gazed with amazement on its vast dimensions and lofty height. Strabo, the Grecian philosopher, beheld its polished sides when the casing stones made them a mirror that flung back the sun's radiance on the green fields of Egypt—beheld in wrapt awe, declaring "IT WAS NOT ERECTED BY MAN'S TOIL, BUT DESCENDED UPON ITS SITE READY FORMED FROM HEAVEN."

Through all the ages this witness, from the dead past to the living present, was silent—made no sign that men could interpret.

The ages moved slowly by. The sand storms swept around its rocky base. Generations after generations rose and gazed and passed away. The Greek and the Roman and the Arab claimed, in turn, to be its owner. It outlived them all, and held its secret until the fulness of its time had come.

At length in the year of our Lord 825, Al Mamoun, a successor of Mahomet, head of the Arabian Empire when it had touched the zenith of its glory, resolved to drag forth the Pyramid's secrets or its treasures into the light.

He had been told by the romancers and fortune tellers of *El Fostat*—the old Cairo—that gold and gems and untold wealth of antediluvian kings were stored in its hidden depths. Secrets too—magic charms, and the wisdom of the golden ages—were treasured in its vast vaults.

Al Mamoun set about the task with the enthusiasm of a fanatic and the cupidity of an ambitious ruler. Relays of workmen inspired by the promises of rich rewards, began to dig into the north side of the Pyramid, just about the same distance from the northeast corner that the real but hidden entrance was, but some forty feet below this. The workmen toiled day and night, week after week even into months, breaking into the solid stone work and blasting in the best way they knew how in that age. Weeks and even months of constant toil gave them no encouragement of piercing the supposed interior hollow where the vast treasures were stored. One hundred feet had been blasted or bored into the stone work, as hard and unyielding as the rocky hillside.

Murmurs arose among the workmen. The command was to dig on. The murmurs of the weary workmen were about to break forth in open refusal and revolt, when an incident occurred of a significant character. The sound of a falling stone revealed a hollow spot next to them. It was announced by the workmen with a shout of cheer. The labors became more hearty. Blows fell quick and heavy, and soon they burst into a " dark hollow place." It was the descending passage seen in the accompanying engraving. It begins fifty feet above the ground, and twenty-four feet east of the center of the northern face of the Pyramid. The Arabs cautiously entered it. They moved up its smooth floor to the entrance, which was filled up either with the original plugs or with broken pieces of the casing stones. Driving out the rock that hid up the mouth of this entrance passage, the sunlight swept down to where the sound of the falling stone had been heard. This was a large stone which fitted into the ceiling with angular shaping, while the face side was smooth and polished and not to be distinguished from the other stones of which

FRONT ELEVATION, *Looking South,*
OF THE ANGLE STONES AND PRESENTLY DILAPIDATED MASONRY,
OVER THE ONE AND SOLE ORIGINAL ENTRANCE PASSAGE INTO THE GREAT PYRAMID.
From a "PHOTOGRAPH *by* P.S."

the ceiling was composed. It had been there, undisturbed since the Pyramid was built. Even if (as is supposed) the descending passage had been entered by its proper mouth or opening in past ages and then this mouth closed up, this stone had never been removed until it was shaken from its position by the blows of Arab hammers.

And now the secret was laid bare. Behind this displaced stone was the evidence of another passage, beginning in the ceiling of this descending one, which slants down over three hundred feet, ending in a vault, or chamber, which is directly under the Pyramid, a hundred feet down in the solid rock.

But the fall of the stone in the ceiling of this descending passage revealed another passage. But its mouth was stopped up with great granite plugs wedged in by the pressure of the stones above, and of such hard material that it was impossible either to shatter or move them. They are there yet. When visiting the Pyramid, one has to climb round or over them through an opening cut in the softer limestone that surrounds these granite wedges which jam up the entrance to this upward passage. Digging their way, the Arabs found the passage, back of the barred entrance, filled up with blocks of limestone. Shattering these with their hammers and lifting them out, others would slide down—another and another—the whole passage, four feet high and three feet wide, filled with blocks of stone nearly as high as the passage itself. Desperate and continued efforts at length removed the last stone. The way was now cleared. The Arabs leaped into this passage, lit up by their glaring torches.

"*Alla Acbar!*" was shouted aloud, — the first sounds and the first foot-falls within those mysterious chambers for three thousand years. All had been blocked up, sealed, hidden from human curiosity since the completion of the massive pile. These stones must have been placed both in the opening of this ascending passage and all up its way when that part of the Pyramid was built. It is impossible that these granite plugs wedged into the lower end of this passage, or the loose stones that filled it all the way up, could have been put there after the Pyramid was completed.

But the way clear, the Arabs, wild with joy, rushed up with bent forms along this four-foot high passage. It soon opened into another one seven times its height, and six feet broad. It was a noble room, with polished marble sides and floor, equal to the finest cabinet work in jointings and finish. Thirty-six great granite blocks span the roof, and seven courses of over-lapping marble slabs form its shining walls. Upright stones bank the sides near the floor, like our wash-boards, in which are found twenty-eight holes at equal distances from each other and above each other. In each of these holes, except the two near the north end and the one in the stone step at the extreme south end, there is set in the wall a vertical stone thirteen inches broad and eighteen high.

The Arabs paused, awe-struck, within this lofty, solemn and mysterious corridor. Their torches could not light up its granite-spanned roof, which appeared twice its real height. Here they expected to find the earnestly-sought treasure, but all was empty, and devoid of any sign or hieroglyphic.

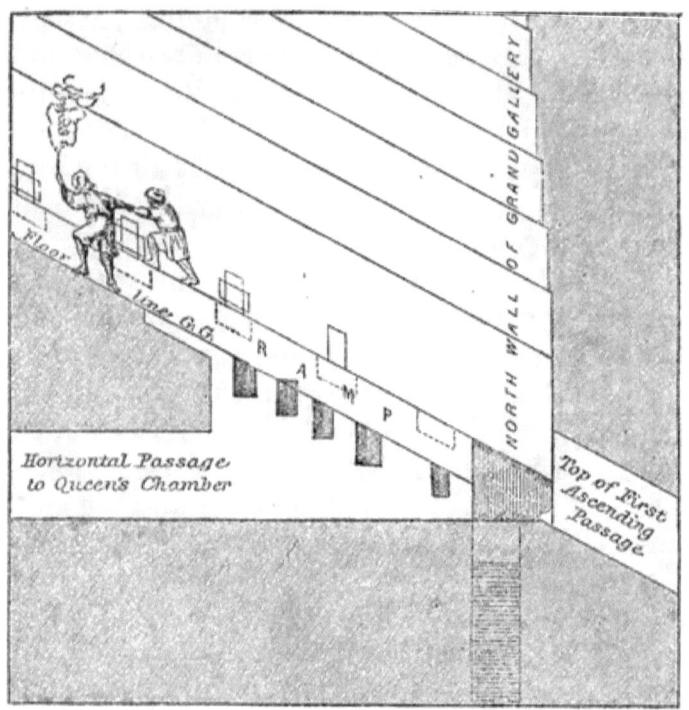

The first entry by the Arabs in the year 825.

On! on! "*Alla Acbar!*" rang out and echoed and re-echoed throughout the length of this wonderful passage. And upward rushed the almost frantic Arabs until they encountered a step, climbing up which they pressed on until met by an impending wall, which suddenly comes down at the south end of the passage and which leaves a narrow one beyond it through which they groped with bended posture until they reached an ante-room, in which is a "granite leaf," as it has been called, and a peculiar protuberance known as the granite "boss." From this they make their way through another low passage overhung by a kind of portcullis— a great granite block resting in grooves, and then with a bound and a shout they stand in a beautiful room now called the King's Chamber, and gaze about them in wonder and disappointment, for this splendid granite room, with its sides polished like the finest jewelry, is empty —treasureless—nothing in it but a great granite chest, hollowed out from a solid rock—lidless, empty, and without a mark or hieroglyphic.

No mummy nor sign of mummy is found in this so-called "sarcophagus," not an inscription on its sides. Not an idolatrous emblem or symbol is traced on the walls of the noble chamber where it rests. Air channels ventilate the room. The immediate entrance to it is open. The granite chest, or coffer, is not built round or closed in. Nothing suggests a coffin, or tomb. No treasures were found in this "sanctuary," for which seemingly the whole mighty fabric was reared. All is silence, emptiness, mystery. "*Alla Acbar!*" again shout the disappointed Arabs, whose work is done, and whose hopes are quenched.

One great fact in regard to the room and its contents is notable. This stone chest or coffer is the size of the ark or chest which God commanded Moses to make and place in it the tablets of the law, the pot of manna, and Aaron's rod that budded—the ark of the covenant, bearing which on their shoulders the priests entered the swollen Jordan and its waters divided so that Israel might pass over dry-shod—the ark, above which was the mercy-seat and the cherubim and the glory of the Shekinah—the ark which typified the Lord Christ. The stone chest or "coffer" found by these intruders into those heretofore sacred and secret chambers was of the dimensions of the ARK OF THE LORD, as will be fully shown farther on.

But to return. The Arabs on entering the long corridor twenty-eight feet high and six feet wide had passed a passage the height of the one that led to it—only four feet. It was horizontal and conducted to a room now called the "Queen's Chamber." This they explored and found entirely empty—with that peculiar niche sunk in the wall showing the sacred cubit, which has already been described. Near the entrance to this horizontal passage is a chasm caused by the absence in this place (or by the tearing away) of one of the bank stones which stand in ranks all up the long corridor. From this hole or chasm a deep channel runs down, ragged and indirect, one hundred and forty feet and meets the descending entrance-passage very near the subterranean vault.

And now the inmost and hitherto secret chambers of this mysterious mountain of stone had been pierced. All was black as night—empty, unlettered, unmeaning. Al Mamoun and his viziers and soldiers stood thunderstruck.

Murmurs were again heard. The Commander of the Faithful was endangered. He met the doubts and demoralization of his faithful followers by burying a certain amount of gold in some part of the Pyramid. The next day he ordered his soldiers to dig at this very spot. They immediately came to the treasure. "Let it be counted!" was the caliph's order. It was carefully counted when "Lo! it amounted to the exact sum that had been spent in the undertaking—neither more nor less. The caliph was astonished and said he could not understand how the kings of the Pyramid could know exactly how much money he would have to expend in work, and he was lost in suprise."

The Arabian poets celebrated his achievement and embellished the story with fables. They gave out that the coffer or stone chest was full of gold, and that a dead man with a breast plate of gold was found in it; all of which are to be classed with the tales of the "Arabian Nights."

But the interior of this "wonder of the ages" was now open for the first time to all men.

And "men did occasionally enter it," says

one of the most reliable historians of the period, "for many years, and descended by the slippery passage which is in it."

But it remained still as barren and meaningless as the desert on whose border it stood. For centuries it was voiceless.

At length in 1637 Professor John Greaves visited the Great Pyramid with a view to study its astronomical bearings and proportions. He was a professor of astronomy in Oxford University. He measured the passages and chambers—but gave more attention to the outside than to the interior. In his published account of his visit and his explorations he pointed out "that Diodorus hath left, above 1,600 years since, a memorable passage concerning Chemmis (Cheops) the builder of the Great Pyramid, and Cephren (Shafre) the royal founder of the work adjoining. 'Although saith he (Diodorus) those kings intended these for their sepulchres, yet it happened that *neither of them was buried there.*'" *

Nearly two hundred years after this work of the old Oxford professor it was again taken up by the engineers and *savants* of Napoleon. Then came Col. Vyse in 1837, expending his time and his fortune in exploration and admeasurements. The general mind was to a great ex-

---

* Greaves, quoted by P. Smyth, "Our Inheritance" p. 129.

tent awakened by his researches. The attention of Sir John Herschel was directed to this memorial of lost science, and finally John Taylor, of London, wrote a work entitled "*Why was the Pyramid Built and Who Built It ?*"

He showed that the shape, the arrangements and other indications of the Great Pyramid proved that its architects possessed profound knowledge of the heavens and of the earth, which Egypt never possessed or even understood, nor any other nation, until a thousand years ago. This work by Taylor arrested the attention of one of the greatest men of this age —Piazzi Smyth, Royal astronomer for Scotland. He resolved, at his own expense to visit the Pyramid. He took with him twenty-seven boxes of instruments by which to make the most accurate observations and measurements. He was assisted by the Egyptian officials—with two *ries* or captains and twenty men from Sakkara to aid in clearing the Pyramid passages and removing obstructions. He measured and re-measured the interior passages and chambers (to which we now direct attention) with the most perfect mathematical instruments. He gave the results to the world in a splendid volume of nearly 700 pages—results which have never been impeached. From these we now proceed to show the sacred symbolisms of the Great Pyramid.

CHAPTER II.

THE DESCENDING PASSAGE — THE DRAGON STAR — THE DOWNWARD DRIFT.

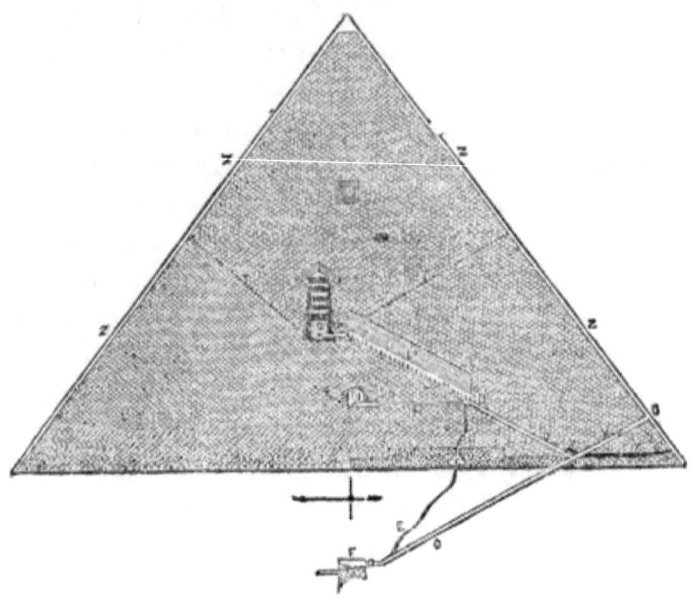

IT will be seen by looking at the chart of the Great Pyramid, that a long slant passage enters the north side of the structure and descends into an angular shaped room one hundred feet down in the solid rock. The ceiling of the subterranean room is " exquisitely smooth." But, as must be presumed, when the original workers had cut downwards from the ceiling to a depth of about four feet to the west and thirteen feet to the east they stopped.

They then bored a hole in the south end and left it unfinished. Then a portion of the bottom was excavated deeper than the other part, and this was also left incomplete. So that the lower part of this room was left in holes and hollows, and on this account has been called "bottomless."

The downward passage to this floorless or "bottomless" underground chamber is 4,404 inches* and is about four feet high and nearly as wide.

This passage is directed to a point in the northern sky 3° 42' below the pole. It will be remembered that the Great Pyramid itself is astronomically oriented—its sides point due north, south, east, and west. But while the side of the structure in which this long descending passage is, points to the pole of the sky, the descending passage points to a spot three degrees and a fraction below it. *Why was this?*

Col. Howard Vyse, concluding that this down-tunnel was built with some astronomical design, submitted to Sir John Herschel the question: "*When did a star shine down that passage, and what was the star?*"

Looking up that long passage into the northern sky a star is seen. It is our present pole star in the constellation of the Little Bear. But that star was not always there. It, like all

---

* According to the measurements of Col. Vyse.

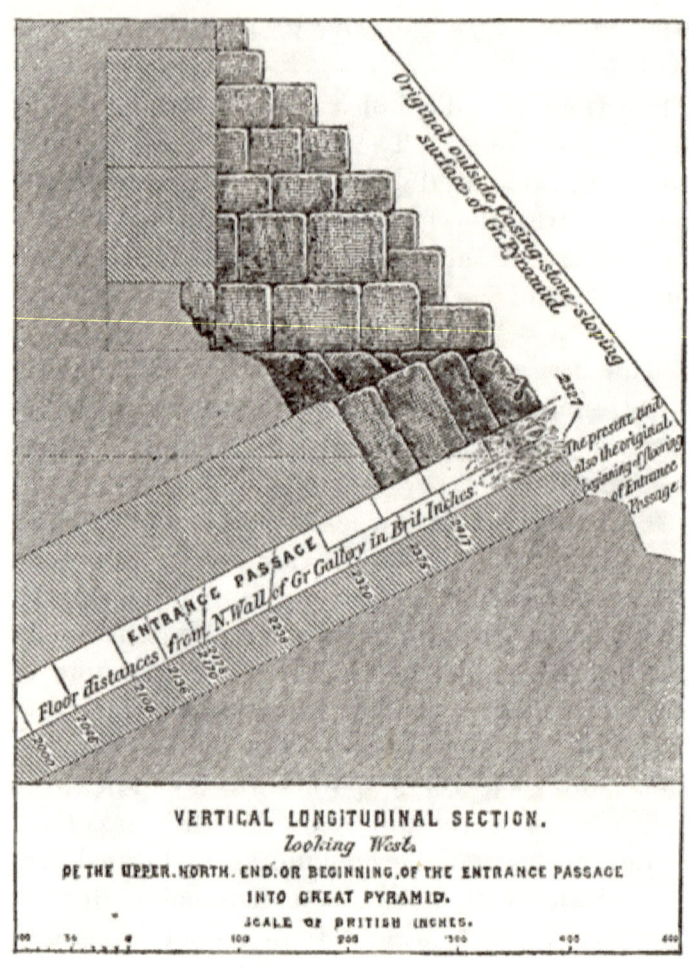

THE DOWNWARD DRIFT.

the other stars and galaxies, moves on in that grand celestial round called the precession of the equinoxes. Now by this "dial of the heavens," the location of any star at any period can be found. Sir John Herschel found that the star Alpha Draconis, when passing below the pole was 3° 42' from the pole of the heavens about 2,170 years before Christ.*

Now here is a *fact* in the construction of the Pyramid which, unless symbolical, is meaningless. An underground floorless or bottomless pit, unfinished and unfit for any earthly practical purpose; a slanting passage-way leading to this subterranean chamber so built that along its whole descent the dragon star looked— built, too, not to point to the true north, but to this particular star when passing below the pole of the heavens. What could more clearly symbolize the terrible facts in human history or human destiny! The progress of humanity, in all that is God-like, has been downward, ever downward. Every age and every people record this downward drift — the *Descensus Averni*. Boast as we may of the civilization and advancement of the race, the stern facts meet us all along the dark and crimsoned march of human-

---

* Professor Proctor, while trying to overthrow the scientific theory of the Great Pyramid says: "Sir John Herschel's correct statement that about the year 2170 B. C. the star *Alpha Draconis* was about 3° 42' from the pole."—*Contemporary Review*.

ity, that in all that bears upon the eternal world, in all that relates to the claims of God over mind and conscience, in all that belongs to true morality, man's way has been downward from the very beginning.

There is nothing more solidly established by science than that the earliest traditions taught this downward drift. According to the Egyptians the terrestial reign of *Ra* was the age of gold. This belief of an age of innocence and bliss by which the career of humanity began is also to be met with among all peoples of Aryan or Japhetic race. The laws of Manu divide the duration of the human race into four ages: the age of perfection (*Kritayuga*); the age of three-fold sacrifice or the accomplishment of all religious duties (*Trêtunga*); the age of doubt or obscuration of religious notions (*Dvaparayuga*); the age of perdition or (*Kaliyuga*) the present age which is to close in the destruction of the world. *

Zoroastrian Mazdeism teaches the same theory. Time is divided into four ages. The first is all pure, like Eden. The good God *Ahuramazda* reigns over his creation in which, as yet, no evil has appeared. In the second age the evil spirit *Angromainyus* issues from the darkness. At first the evil spirit has com-

---

* François Lenormant, in *Contemporary Review*, Sept. 1, 1870.

paratively little power. Finally during historic times he prevails, but his defeat is accomplished and the evil of this last age is to be followed by the resurrection of the dead and the beatitude of the risen just.* The laws of Manu say with this decline in religion and morality there is a steady decrease in the length of human life—in the proportion of 4, 3, 2, 1. And then the evil spirit is represented as the serpent, the dragon, who is the god of this world.

The inspired record of the fall through the promptings of the old serpent is echoed in the scriptures of Zoroastrianism in these words: "I created the first and best of dwelling places (Eden). I who am Ahuramazda; the Airyana Vædja is of excellent nature. But against it Angromainyus, the murderer, created a thing inimical, the serpent out of the river and the winter, the work of the Dœvas (demons.)" *

This scourge caused by the power of the serpent drives men out of the best of dwelling places.

These quotations are introduced to show that before the written word, before the inspired record of man's fall and downward drift, *the facts* were recorded in human memory and symbolized in these myths.

---

* Theopompus, cited by the author of the "Treatise on Isis and Osiris." (Plutarch, C. 47).
† "Yesht," 19. "Bundehesh," 23.

A cylinder of hard stone is preserved in the British Museum dug up from ruins in Assyria and of great antiquity, on which are seen the outlines of a man and a woman seated opposite each other on either side of a tree from whose spreading branches two big fruits hang, one in front of each of the figures, who are stretching out their hands to gather it. A serpent is rearing himself up behind the woman.*

"The existence of this tradition," says the author already quoted, "in the cycle of the indigenous legends of the Canaanites, seems to me placed beyond doubt, by a curious painted vase of Phenician workmanship of the seventh or sixth century before Christ, discovered by General di Cesnola in one of the most ancient sepulchres of Idalia, in the Isle of Cyprus. There we see a leafy tree, from the branches of which hang two large clusters of fruit, while a great serpent is advancing with undulating movements towards the tree and rearing itself to seize hold of the fruit."

And so the sacred books of Ancient India, like the poetry of Hesiod, show that it was by the law of decadence and deterioration that the ancient world believed itself so heavily laden. "In proportion as time passed and things departed further and further from their point of emanation, they corrupt themselves and grow worse and worse."

---

* Lenormant, C. R., p. 54.

Now, these traditions or beliefs, originating in the *facts* recorded in the Bible, and seen in an "evolution of decline" towards idolatry and barbarism, savagery and beastly degradation, could not be more clearly and strikingly symbolized in stone than they are in this downward passage along which the light of the dragon star gleamed, and which ended in the deep, dark, floorless pit.

The existence of an evil principle, of a personal and powerful agency controlling the race in this decadence, is embraced in universal tradition, is felt in universal experience, and is the only solution of the problem of evil. But the existence of this evil one is taught in God's inspired word. He is called the "Prince of the power of the air," "the spirit that now worketh in the children of disobedience." He is called "the God of this world," and "the world lieth in the wicked one." He is called "the Dragon," "the old serpent," and is declared to be a tempter, liar, murderer, destroyer, to whose usurped power men slavishly yield. Under his influence it is declared "evil men shall wax worse and worse." And that "as in the days of Noah, and in the days of Lot, so shall it be at the end of this age—in the days of the Son of Man." Then, and not till then, shall this dragon power "fall like lightning from the heavens and be given to the burning flame."

CHAPTER III.

SACRED TIME MEASURES — FROM BABEL TO SINAI.

THIS downward passage, as has been described in the foregoing chapter, is met by another one running in the same southward direction, but upwards. It strikes the ceiling of the downward one, and is walled up with hard stone wedges, and was found filled up with large, loose stones. As the explorer goes down the slippery floor of the downward way, he notices these wedges are placed in the original entrance to this other and upward way. The Arabs, as already stated, cut away the softer side stones so as to get round and above these plugs. It is still reached by climbing up this "cut-off."

By the measurements of Col. Vyse,* and the still more accurate measurements of Professor Smyth, it is found that the beginning of this ascending passage is 988 inches from the mouth of the long descending passage, and leads into a still higher and longer one.

---

* The author has carefully examined and compared Howard Vyse's measurements with those of the Astronomer Royal.

The question has been asked, "Why this seeming change in the plan of the Pyramid? Why this sudden turn in the entrance passage? Why this difference in the interior from all the lesser and later pyramids? The main descending passage was planned with astronomical precision. It was leveled at the Dragon star. It entered the subterranean room a hundred feet directly under the Pyramid. What use was there for any other passages? Was the first plan abandoned and the lower room left unfinished, and this other passage built in the structure to lead to chambers better suited to the object of the builders than the subterranean vault could be?

These questions have been answered in the affirmative by rationalistic Egyptologists, but without a particle of proof.

Dr. S. Birch, in a learned work on the "Discoveries in Egypt," conjectures *why* these supposed alterations were made. By comparing his language with the account obtained from the Egyptian priest through an interpreter, and recorded by Herodotus, it will be seen that Dr. Birch has no information to impart except what we have already quoted from Herodotus. After giving in substance what is related by that author, he guesses why the lower vault was abandoned, and this ascending passage made to lead into the interior chambers.

The following is Dr. Birch's language:

"It is by far the most remarkable of all the

pyramids, for several changes appear to have taken place during its construction. The first or nobler chamber appears to have been abandoned in consequence of the prolongation of the passage extending beyond the base, the Pyramid having continued to be built for a longer time than originally contemplated. A second chamber, called the Queen's, with a pointed roof, was then made in the masonry of the Pyramid 67 feet above the level of the base, and had a horizontal passage for 110 feet in the masonry communicating with the original passage, sloping at an angle with it. Finally the King's Chamber, or main one, the last made with flat roof and five chambers of construction placed above, the last triangular to lighten the weight of the masonry, was approached by the same passage as the Queen's Chamber, much enlarged and cased with red Syenitic granite, terminating in a horizontal passage with granite port-cullises, which were also to defend the entrance. This chamber was ventilated by two shafts, and had in the centre the plain but royal sarcophagus of the builder of the Pyramid. The stones of the chambers of construction had still scrawled in red ochre upon them the name of Khrum Khufa, or Cheops, accompanied by other marks which the masons had scrawled upon them in the quarries. *

---

* Page 113.

But over against these *guesses* stands the *fact that matured plan* marks every step in the progress and completion of the gigantic pile. Supposing that the underground vault was abandoned, and therefore left in its strange unfinished condition, the change would be decided on before the vast layers of masonic stone were piled one upon another to the height of fifty feet. But then the ascending passage, to take the place of the one cut down in the bed-rock, would have been commenced at once and so as to lead directly to the interior chamber, which on the supposition that it was decided to build it, after the underground vault was abandoned. But this was not done. The descending passage is built in the masonry up to fifty feet above the foundation. Its entrance is that number of feet from the original pavement. Why was this passage built up in the structure to this height if the plan of the subterranean vault had been abandoned? It would not have been thus continued, but instead of it a passage would have been formed direct from the pavement into the interior chamber, which was to be reached (on this supposition of a change in the plan) instead of the underground vault. The evidence is then, in the complete construction of the passages, that, the ascending passage, which starts out of the descending one was acccording to the original plan of these scientific architects. And then the question comes up, "*Why ?*" There is no conceivable reason for this downward and then this upward passage unless to symbolize some great facts or scrolls of human history.

What facts, then, or scrolls of history, are of sufficient importance, or bear such relation to human destiny, as to be worth a record in changeless symbols in the "oldest and most gigantic of human works?"

Was there a period in the history of the race marking an ascent from the downward drift of humanity to a knowledge of the moral law or to a knowledge of the true God? It will be answered by even the skeptic that such an event took place when the people of Israel passed from slavery and ignorance and idolatry to freedom, and written law and moral culture and the worship of the one holy God—when they left Egypt for Canaan.

Whatever may be the doubts of men with regard to the miracles and the divine interposition connected with the exodus of the Hebrews from Egypt, all acknowledge that it was an advance and upward movement, and that it affected the current of history for all time. Its effects, after nearly four thousand years have elapsed, are felt by every nation under heaven to-day. Was this world-crisis of sufficient importance to be symbolized by an ascent from the downward way leading to the confused, floorless and, as it is termed, "bottomless pit," adown which the eye of the Dragon Star gleamed?

Now let it be observed that this upward passage is 988 inches from the beginning of the downward one—just about the number of years (so far as chronology can determine the exact number) intervening between the dispersion of the tribes of men at Babel's tower and the going up of Israel out of Egypt.

That dispersion, with the confusion of tongues, is significant of universal world-history.

"The account," says Lange, "of the building of the Tower of Babel may be regarded as the genesis of the history of the human race, striving after a false unity; of the doom of confusion that God, therefore, imposed upon it; of the dispersion of the nations into all the world, and of the formation of heathendom as directly connected therewith."

"Go to, let us build a tower for US, and make to ourselves A NAME." It was a Titanic, heaven-defying undertaking; and from it sprang the heathen fable of the war of giants against the gods. The very name Nimrod (which is in the first person plural) signifies "*come let us*"—REBEL. "Its grammatical force shows that it had a popular, instead of a family, origin. It was the watchword of the impious leader afterwards given to him by his applauding followers." But on the God-defying hosts fell the scattering and confounding blow. On the summit of all their defiant pride was written a sudden and strange defeature. "A confounding of languages presupposes a confusion of consciousness in respect to God and the world. The history of the tower-builders is the history of the origin of heathenism." *

Now this downward course of man—just after the judgment of the deluge, and the rainbow, symbol of mercy—had its marked starting-point *about* one thousand years before the exodus of Israel from Egypt. The word "about" is here used because there is much of uncertainty in regard to historic dates. Bible chronology is based on the lives of the patriarchs rather than the occurrence of historic events. Hence the difficulties in forming correct chronological tables, as will be seen from the following list:

Authorities.	Date of Deluge
Septuagint	B. C. 3246.
Samaritan	" 2998.
Jackson	" 3170.
R. S. Pool	" 3129.
W. Osburn (Monumental History of Egypt)	" 2500.
Elliot's *Horæ Apocalipticæ*	" 2482.
Browne's *Ordo Sæculorum*	" 2446.
Playfair	" 2351.
Usher	" 2348.
Petavius (Smith's Bible Dic.)	" 2327.

It is difficult to come to any conclusion when such a wide divergence is found in results

---

* Fabri's "Origin of Heathendom," p. 39.

which must have followed years of careful research by men fully competent to the task. What then is the best (or it may be said) only safe method to pursue when so many different dates of one event meet us ? Let us take the mean (or average) of the whole, thus striking a balance between 3246 years and the lowest date, 2327. Now the mean or average date is 2741, and strange to say the Pyramid's chronological measurements symbolize this very number. It is quite evident that the dispersion did not take place until about two hundred years after the flood. "I make the beginning of idolatry, and the consequent dispersion, to have occurred about 200 years after the flood.* This would make the date of the dispersion (according to the average above given) 2541 years before Christ. The exodus, by the more recent investigations, occurred over 1500 B. C. Now counting from the beginning of the entrance passage to the beginning of the ascending one, the inches bring out this very date (as we shall see). In other words, counting back from the ascending passage 988 inches, and taking these as an inch for a year, we find a number coming within a fraction of the date of that grand epoch—the confusion of tongues and the dispersion of the tribes. The last results of chronological study make that date 2541 years before Christ. The Pyramid meas-

---

* Jones' "Hist. Church of God," p. 7.

uring makes it 2530 before Christ or 988 years before the exodus.

A thousand inches (nearly) from the commencement of that downward way along which the Dragon Star shone, there is a sudden and marked ascent. This is the fact in the Pyramid to-day—utterly purposeless unless it was intended as a symbol. But here is the fact in the world-history. A thousand years (nearly) from the commencement of the downward drift of humanity under the influence of the Dragon—the serpent-devil—and there was an ascent. A portion of the downward drifting race was lifted up from the dehumanizing abominations, the bestial idolatry, in which all the tribes of men gloried—were lifted by a mighty arm, by prodigy and miracle, by cloud and flame pillar—were called to hear the voice of the Eternal and receive his written law from the lightning-girt summit of Sinai, trembling before the presence of the I AM.

The fact that the Hebrew nation had drifted into abasing calf-worship, and bestial degradation in their slavery to the worshipers of the ox, and the ape, and the crocodile, is denied by none. The fact that they were delivered from all this, to a purer and loftier plane of religion and morals and manners, is nowhere denied. There stood Israel through succeeding centuries—the lighthouse in a world of gloom—rooted on the rock of truth, while the nations of the earth drifted on, on to darkness and perdition.

Standing by itself, with no other features or parallels, *synchronizing* important eras both as to beginnings and endings — from what they spring and to what they led — this *apparent* symbolism might seem far-fetched or fanciful. But when there are added to all this the mechanical data next to be noticed, the wonderful agreement of inches with years in movements of providential history fills us with conviction and awe.

The conclusion is thus forced on the mind, that this epoch in the history of the race, the call of Israel from Egypt with all its bearings upon the religious thought, culture and destiny of humanity, is memorialized both in regard to its date and continuance in this vast monument, "a sign, and a witness to the Lord in the midst of the land of Egypt."

CHAPTER IV.

FROM EGYPT TO BETHLEHEM.

NINE hundred and eighty-eight inches from this descending passage, which leads to the subterranean pit, and down which the Dragon Star looked, is the ascending passage— the way of escape from the downward way. Nine hundred and eighty-eight years (or, in round numbers, one thousand years) after the dispersion, occurred the exodus from Egypt. This passage, accurately measured from the floor of the ascending one up to the ceiling and then along to where it ends in a still longer, higher and grander one, is just 1542 inches.

It has been shown in the first part of this volume that an inch for a year, in the two longest lines in the Pyramid—the added diagonals— measure the great precessional cycle of 25,827 years. It has been shown that from the beginning of the downward passage to the beginning of this ascending one is equal, an inch for a year, to the time from the dispersion to the time Israel left Egypt. And now here is another wonderful coincidence (as many term it), viz: the length of this ascending passage is equal, an inch for a year, to the time from the exodus from Egypt to the birth of Christ.

Usher's Chronology dates the exodus 1491 years before Christ. This, says the learned editor of Lange's Commentary, is usually set down in round numbers 1500 years. But that writer tells us that it was several years more than this. The Rev. W. B. Galloway, M. A., Vicar of St. Mark's, Regent's Park, London, in a work entitled "Egypt's Record of Time to the Exodus of Israel," makes the date of the exodus 1542 years before Christ.* Now the exact measure of this ascending passage from the floor of the downward one to where the long high corridor begins, is exactly 1542 inches. The precise measure of the Jewish dispensation is thus marked in clearest symbolism in the length of this ascent.

But more than this: the passage itself, as has been shown, is blocked up with hard immovable granite wedges. Why? There was no apparent object for this. But as a symbol it corresponds with the Jewish dispensation. That people were not only lifted from the downward drift but were sealed. God chose them as His own "peculiar people." No one can be a Jew unless the blood of Abraham courses his veins. God separated them from the nations of the earth and distinguished them physically, mentally and in all their characteristics from every

---

* "Egypts Record," p. 371. He also proved that the birth of our Savior occurred, according to our reckoning, only within a fraction of the year B. C. 1.

other people under heaven. They have been supernaturally wedged in, nationally, as effectually as that passage is literally.

This itself is a living miracle. If a handful of water taken from one of our inland streamlets were flung into the Mississippi and borne to the Gulf and across the Atlantic and swept through seas and oceans, by wind and wave round the earth, and yet every drop retained its own freshness and consistency, unchanged and unaltered by rushing currents or crushing waves, it would be no greater miracle than that God should have taken a handful of people out of Egypt and cast them upon the tides of humanity, to be scattered abroad over earth through centuries, and yet remain distinct from all other peoples—a Jew proud of his lineage and name wherever found or driven. How significantly is this symbolized by the blocking up with immovable granite rocks, the entrance to this 1542 inch passage!

Another peculiarity about this ascending passage is, that at its beginning, and in other portions to be mentioned, the tunnel is cut through a huge block of stone, so that floor, walls and ceiling are formed by the one piece. The passage is nearly four feet high and three and a half feet wide, and passes through stone after stone, fitted closely together, through which the square passage-way has been cut. These plates at the entrance, cut clean through, extend to the length of 253 inches from the floor of the descending passage. Beyond this the walls, floor and ceiling are built, for some distance at least, with regularly *jointed* stones. Here then at the beginning this passage is hollowed out of great blocks of rock. Is there anything in the commencement of the Mosaic dispensation—which lasted in years the length of this passage—which these *plates* of stone can symbolize? We know that God girded and sheltered Israel and bore them up with His providence and His mighty hand for centuries after they left Egypt. In the wilderness, under Joshua and the Theocracy, God was their strength and their rock of defense. What could more fittingly symbolize this than that this passage at its beginning should be girded by the plates of stone so cut through, that floor, wall and ceiling should be of one unbroken piece? These plates are again found far up the passage, and answer in inches to the years of David and Solomon's reigns. Then another portion follows with jointed stones. But at that number of inches which corresponds to the years of Hezekiah and other pious kings, these massive girding plates form the way. And at the number of inches distant from the beginning of the passage, which equals the years when the voice of prophecy was silent—amounting to 400 years— there *are none* of those rock girders for 400 inches up to the end of the passage. These *may* be only singular coincidences, but how wonderful that they should follow each other with pointed and almost speaking significance!

In addition to the distances that these protecting plates are placed, marking an inch for a year, in Jewish history, it was found by the measurement of a competent civil engineer that the intervals of passage length at which these remarkable stone plates were introduced, were the breadths of the central room in the building called the King's Chamber. This chamber in its breadth was the standard of measure in these significant safety plates, indicating that the more glorious periods in the Jewish dispensation, marked by massive bored rocks, were prophecies of a still more glorious period, when the "*king* shall reign in righteousness."

In viewing this first ascending passage, we find these facts with their corresponding symbolisms. First, we have its beginning, 1000 inches (nearly) from the beginning of the downward passage, and the exodus of the Jews from Egypt took place 1000 years nearly from the "dispersion" at Babel's tower; then we have the blocked-up mouth, symbolizing the Jewish nation sealed and kept by the providence of God; and then we find these solid plates of stone answering, as we have shown, to the special blessings of God to that nation when it acknowledged His rule; and then we find it ending at the close of 1542 inches, the length in years of the Jewish dispensation, or from the exodus to the birth of Christ, when it leads into a grand corridor or gallery of seven-fold its height.

Are not these facts significant? What shall we think of them? Meet them with a shrug of the shoulder or a scornful sneer? There stands the Pyramid with these shapings and constructions and measurements in themselves purposeless, and there are the facts of history—traditions the skeptic may call them—fitting into these measurements or symbols like the tongue and groove of a piece of refined mechanism. Does it not appear that these historic facts affecting human weal through time and eternity were stamped on this gigantic pile in that morning of humanity as a witness for God to men in this scoffing, doubting age, "a sign and a witness to the Lord in the land of Egypt?"

CHAPTER V.

THE GRAND CORRIDOR AND GOSPEL ERA—THE DISRUPTED ROCK, AND THE RESURRECTION OF JESUS.

The Missing Ramp-stone.

THE ascending passage, with all its wonderful symbolism, ends 1542 inches from the floor of the downward one, in a lofty corridor or gallery, twenty-eight feet high and a little over six feet wide. As the visitor emerges from the first ascending way, in which he has to bend down, it being but four feet high, he feels, with the relief of an upright position, that he is in a room arranged with some noble design. It is built of, or rather cased in with, pure marble. The joints are needle-proof, and though cemented can scarcely be seen. The roof, twenty-eight feet high, is spanned with thirty-six great granite blocks, between which plates of marble form the polished ceiling. All along the sides of this princely corridor are ranges of marble slabs overlapping so as to make the passage narrower at the floor than at the ceiling. No marble hall can be found on earth surpassing it in beauty of finish or mechanical skill.

Professor Greaves two hundred years ago described it as "a very stately piece of work, and not inferior either in respect of the curiosity of art or richness of materials to the most sumptuous and magnificent buildings." "This gallery or corridor," continues the old Oxford professor, "or whatsoever else I may call it, is built of white and polished marble, the which is very evenly cut in spacious squares or tables. Of such materials as is the pavement such is the roof and such are the side walls that flank it. The coagmentation or knitting of the joints is so close that they are scarcely discernible to a curious eye. And that which adds grace to the whole structure, though it makes the passage the more slippery and difficult, is the acclivity and rising of the ascent. The gallery is bounded on both sides with two banks like benches of sleek and polished stone. Upon the top of these benches, near the angle where they close and join the wall, are little spaces cut in right-angled parallel figures, set on each side opposite one another, intended, no question, for *some other end than ornamentation.*"

"In the casting and ranging of the marbles in both the side walls there is one piece of architecture in my judgment very graceful, and that is that all the courses or ranges, which are but seven, do set and flag over one another about three inches, the bottom of the uppermost course overflagging the top of the next, and so in order the rest as they descend." *

Colonel Vyse, two hundred years after the foregoing was written, gave to the world a very similar description of the grand corridor, calling the bench, or bank stones, "ramps." Every visitor verifies these statements. There is that noble gallery, with those "stone benches," or "ramps," opposite one another, "*intended, no question, for other purposes than ornamentation.*"†

What could these "other purposes than ornamentation" be?

Richard A. Proctor accounted for them, "*a priori,*" as he termed it, as made for seats for

---

* Greaves' Work, edited by Dr. Birch, 1737.
† *Contemporary Review,* Vol. 1, No. 3, p. 39.

star-gazers, who took their positions in this ascending grand gallery before the structure had been built up any higher. He imagined a quantity of water poured into the descending passage. This water would be a mirror just at the corner where the entrance is met by the ascending passage. "The observer, sitting on those slanting benches, would look down the one passage and see Alpha Draconis by rays reflected in the water."

A most scientific guess, assuredly. The astronomers sit on stone benches, which incline, facing each other, what for? They could have gone down into the passage which was leveled at Alpha Draconis and observe it to their hearts' content. But instead of this they are to sit fronting each other and look down into a dish of water to see the star by reflection, and this when the star was *known* to be directly along the line of the ascending passage. To build this passage with all its elaborate finish for such a temporary and useless purpose would be ridiculous. And the credulity of the scientist who can believe that this was the purpose of these stone benches is marvelous.

But let it be observed—

1st, This grand corridor commences at the close of the 1542-inch gallery. That 1542-inch gallery agrees in its symbolism of length and construction with the length and peculiarities of the Mosaic dispensation. At the close of that dispensation the revelation of the Son of

God from heaven took place—1542 years after the exodus of Israel from Egypt.

2d, This grand corridor is twenty-eight feet high, seven times the height of the 1542-inch ascending passage. Seven we know is the number of *perfection*—as "seven spirits," "seven churches," "seven angels," "seven years," etc. The gospel dispensation was the perfection of Judaism. It is called "the glory that surpasseth." Of the dispensation of the law it is written, "For even that which was made glorious had no glory in this respect by reason of the glory that excelleth." Glorious as is the 1542-inch ascending passage, with its massive tunneled plates, it has no glory in this respect "by reason of the glory that excelleth" in this grand gallery. Seven, the number of perfection, marks its walls up to its termination, by the seven courses of over-lapping marble plates on each side from floor to ceiling, as well as its seven-fold height.

3d, Thirty-three inches from its beginning, where the first of those "stone benches" or "ramps" would be found, is a yawning hole, so formed that it should appear as though the ramp stone had been uprooted, or burst up and out from beneath. That it was thus driven out from beneath, or made to appear so, is evident from the fact that a portion of the adjoining stone has been torn away with it.

The absence of this first "ramp stone" has

been accounted for in this way. The workmen having plugged up the ascending passage leading to this grand corridor, had no way of escape but down this hole. They therefore, after filling up the ascending passage with great stones, descended through this narrow, uneven way almost down to the subterranean vault, and then up the long descending passage to the outlet. But would not these masterly architects and workmen have found it easier to have blocked up or filled with rocks that ascending passage as they were building upwards, especially as the hole must deform the otherwise symmetrical and highly finished corridor? But if they overlooked all this as the building progressed upward, how easy for such skilful workmen as the gallery shows them to have been, to fit a slab of stone over the way of escape and as the last man descended let it fall into its place, and thus preserve the completeness of the whole plan.

In fact, if the plugs and great stones filling up the ascending passage were not put there before the structure was built any higher, they could not have been put there at all. It would have been impossible for the workmen to fill in these great stones in the passage after it was built up to its full height. But if the wedges and great blocks of stone were put in the passage as the work went on, then there was no occasion for the workmen to escape anywhere. In any view of the case the way, Col. Vyse and others account for this missing ramp stone and the yawning hole is unreasonable.

No, there is no explanation of this missing stone—nor, indeed, of those still standing—unless it be that it symbolized some great event.

Now it is convincingly significant of this that just thirty-three pyramid inches from the beginning of this seven-fold corridor—thirty-three inches from the end of the 1542-inch passage—occurs this disrupted "ramp stone," as a part too, of the plan of the symmetrically constructed apartment.

There is the fact, unaccountable unless intended as a symbol.

Then here is the historic fact that fits it. Thirty-three years from the birth of Jesus, announced by the choral melody of the angels, He was crucified, His body laid in the stony crypt, where all earth's hopes lay buried with Him. But He could not be held in death's grasp. "He burst the marble jaws of death." He rose in triumph from the grave, and triumphantly placed above it the standard inscribed with His and His people's watchword—" I AM THE RESURRECTION AND THE LIFE."

Thirty-three years from Christ's birth in the stable was His resurrection from the tomb; Thirty-three inches from the beginning of the grand corridor is this chasm left open by the burst-up stone. The four-foot-high passage merges in the seven-fold one, up to this mouth of the chasm. For thirty-three inches it is lost in the corridor. Then comes this well's mouth, where the stone has been driven out from beneath. After this the same four-foot-high ascending passage is traced again—emerging at the left of the grand corridor, in a horizontal direction, into what is called the Queen's Chamber. And the Mosaic dispensation was merged in the dawn of the new dispensation while Jesus was on earth, yet remained under the law. Thirty-three years from his birth, and the vail of the temple was rent in twain and the line of demarkation was drawn. If the four-foot-high passage—whose length, 1542 inches, measures the years of the Mosaic dispensation — symbolizes the Jewish people, then from the resurrection of Jesus the Christ they go on with no farther ascent until their destiny as a people shall be fulfilled. The horizontal passage will be noticed in the chart of the interior of the Pyramid. It will be observed that it strikes off in a straight line from the chasm or well's mouth where the stone has been forced up. How perfect this symbolism! Since the resurrection of Jesus, there has been no advance in Judaism. The Jews were in numbers then just about what they number to-day. They had their Sadducees and Pharisees then, they have their orthodox and reformed Jews now —the latter ritualistic theists. Towards the end of this four-foot-high horizontal passage — whose height and breadth are the same as the first ascending passage—the floor is lower. That lowest section is just *one-seventh* of the whole length, marking one peculiarity of the Jews—their adherence, nominally at least, to the seventh day, and perhaps indicating also the people's lower religious plane, as the years go on.

Then comes the so-called Queen's Chamber. Two air tubes have been discovered in it. They had been covered in by the builders, as though intended to symbolize the blindness of that people. These air passages have not been traced to the exterior and may symbolize something in their history not yet understood at this date.

This was the chamber of sevens. Its two-sided ceiling added to its floor and four walls, makes it a seven-sided room, with other sevens indicated in its measurements. This chamber doubtless symbolizes a future of restoration and glory to that people whom God ennobled and called up from the degrading idolatry of Egypt, and whom he sealed and has kept through all the mutations of centuries for some future privileges and blessings.

From this disrupted ramp stone, just thirty-three inches from the beginning of the corridor, and from which starts out the continuation of the 1542-inch-long passage, begin the ranks of stone-like benches opposite each other all the way up the sides of this avenue.

Each one of these—as noticed by Professor Greaves two hundred years ago, and again by

Col. Vyse in 1837, and fully described with their measurements by Professor Smyth, and to be seen by all who visit the Pyramid — has lateral holes cut "near the angle where they close and join the wall." These, as the old Oxford professor said, "*were intended for some other end than ornamentation.*"

They must have been intended as symbols—to teach something. But what do these spaces cut in these "stone benches" resemble, but graves—the end and rest of all living? Each of these stones (except the two lower and upper ones) is marked by a piece of stone about thirteen inches broad and eighteen inches high, let into the wall uprightly.*

As nothing could better symbolize in stone the *rest* of the grave than those side-long holes, cut at intervals in the stone benches or ramps so nothing could better symbolize in stone the *resurrection* from the grave, than these upright stones let into the wall above them.

The resurrection of Christ is the central and crowning doctrine of the gospel. "If Jesus be not raised your faith is vain, ye are yet in your sins," "then they also who are fallen asleep in Christ are perished." † It was the most important event in the annals of the universe. If that "oldest and most gigantic work of human hands" was built for no other end than to sym-

---

* Smyth's "Our Inheritance," etc., p. 453.
† 1 Cor. 15 : 17, 18.

bolize this one occurrence, it would have been worthy of all the skill, science, labor and expense lavished upon the mighty structure. It is evidently symbolized there in this grand corridor, just thirty-three inches from the termination of the passage which fitly symbolizes the Jewish dispensation. And then from this symbol of the grave and resurrection, commence these side-long holes — these little grooves, backed by the upright stones indicating a rising up. Christ's resurrection is the spring and the pledge of the resurrection of His people. "Because He lives we shall live also." "He hath begotten us again unto a lively hope by the resurrection of Jesus Christ from the dead."* This *lively* or living hope of our resurrection springing from His, is the light that shines all along the ranks of God's struggling hosts. "For if we believe that Jesus died and rose again, even them also which sleep in Jesus will God bring with him."† And so Paul considered the whole gospel bound up in this, when he said in his defense before Agrippa, "of the hope of the resurrection of the dead I am called in question."‡

To quench this hope, to undermine this doctrine, rationalists and skeptics and false professors direct their most ingenious efforts and

---

* I Peter 1 5.
† I Thess. 4 : 14.
‡ Acts 23 : 6.

aim their heaviest blows. It is assailed by philologists, and physiologists, and biologists, and scientists of every form and grade, while it is let alone, if not denied by a sensational or perfunctory ministry. But there stands this foundation-doctrine, this glorious hope, in towering prominence in *God's Word;* and there stands the symbol of this foundation doctrine, this glorious hope, in towering prominence in *the Pyramid*— in this seven-fold gallery. The upright stones lie back of, and rise above the ramp stones— the resurrection hope over the gloom of the grave.

And yet even physiology and biology show that the waste, or loss or change of the particles of matter composing our bodies, has nothing to do with corporeal manhood. Each one of us is the same man, the same woman, though now possessing no particle of the matter in his or her body which composed it a few years ago. These particles, the whole materials which made up our bodies a few years since, have gone into other organisms—are scattered to the four winds—yet we are the same men and women we were before these mutations. And what if in the resurrection there is not found one particle of the matter which composed our bodies when we died? Will this in any way affect the reality of our identical manhood?

The dead shall be raised at the coming of our Lord, and we who are left over and are alive at His coming shall be changed, and so shall we be forever with the Lord. This is the completion of that perfection of Judaism—the end of our salvation.

Then as the corridor is *seven times* the height of the 1542-inch gallery which precedes it—the symbol of perfection—and as sevens are marked all up its sides in the seven over-lapping ranges of marble plates, so there are four times seven of these little graves cut in the top of the bench stones, or "ramps." Four we know is the sign of completion. The *four* living creatures in Ezekiel's vision and also in the Apocalypse denote the complete number of the saved ones. The terrible and continuous wrath visited upon the Jews is called *four* sure judgments on Jerusalem. The impious world-power is figured as *four* beasts. And so we read of *four* angels who sound their trumpets as symbolizing the completion of Earth's woes.* And so, also, the white, the red, the black and the pale horses—*four*, symbolizing the calamities which precede the opening of the fifth seal.

Here then is evidence, without any straining, that the number *four* stands for completion, as *seven* does for perfection. And so the grand gallery, or corridor, is *four* times *seven*. It has *seven* over-lapping stone courses all along its sides up to *four* times seven feet in height, and it has *four* times seven of these *graves* cut in

---

* Rev. 8 : 7 8.

its *four* times *seven* bench or ramp stones, with the upright stones rising over them. Could these stones preach more plainly — could these truths be more impressedly engraved in monumental marble? Four times seven meet us at every point in the splendid corridor, like signatures of the divine hand that His work is perfect, His plans complete, and testifying to the completeness of His perfect work, when the blessed dead who die in the Lord "shall live and reign with Christ on earth a thousand years." "*This is the first resurrection.*" *

How that grand gallery witnesses unto the Lord! All along its ceiling are great granite blocks binding and sheltering it. They are thirty-six in number—equal to the months in the public and vicarious ministry of Jesus. These thirty-six protecting granite blocks—the beams of this mysterious chamber—harmonize in number with its cubic contents. The gallery contains, by the most exact calculations, thirty-six millions of cubic inches, being one million for each one of the thirty-six roof-stones. The measure of the Holy City, which John saw coming down from heaven: which with *four* square was "twelve times twelve thousand furlongs," † that is, 144,000. This was also the number of those John saw standing with the Lamb on

---

* Rev., 20.
† Vatican Manuscript. Rev. 7 : 4.

Mount Zion—144,000. Now this measure of the Celestial City, 144,000 furlongs, brought over in cubits (250 cubits in a furlong), make thirty-six million cubits. The symbolized measure of the Holy City is therefore given in the Apocalypse, 36,000,000 cubits; and the contents of this grand gallery are 36,000,000 inches.

"*Everything is mysterious,*" wrote the French Academician years ago; "I REPEAT IT, everything is mysterious in the construction and distribution of this monument—the passages, oblique, horizontal, sharply bent, of different dimensions. We are not at all enlightened," he continues, "either upon the origin, or the employment, the utility, *or any motive for the grand gallery or its various passages.*"

Yet this most elaborate and closely-calculated design is stamped upon all adjustments and proportions of the Pyramid. It is now acknowledged by all thinking men that it was built for astronomical observations, or memorializations. It stands on the line of 30° latitude. It is placed in the center of the habitable land distribution of the earth. It has such angles, such height and such breadth of base as practically to solve the most profound problems in mathematics and astronomy. Could it be that the architects who planned on such scientific principles the vast structure, would form the grand gallery, with all its skilful workmanship, all its elaborate finish, all its harmonious arrangements, with no purpose, no object in view as to "*its employment, utility or any motive?*"

In all else but its symbolization it is useless and worthless and meaningless. Only as a parable in stone could its wise, scientific architects have planned it. Its symbolism once admitted and it becomes a volume whose leaves of polished stone testify for God to this drifting infidel age—testify to the glorious plan of the redemption of a ruined world.

CHAPTER VI.

THE GOSPEL SYMBOLISM OF THE GRAND CORRIDOR—A PARABLE IN STONE.

WE have seen that thirty-three inches from the north wall or beginning of the grand gallery is the yawning chasm, or mouth of "a strange well," where the ramp stone has been burst up from beneath. This so-called well, or *souterrain*, as it is also termed, runs down through the masonry and through the original rock (which in this place was left standing and forms a part of the structure). Nearly half way down it expands into a bowl-shaped grotto. It continues its ragged and irregular course till it meets the main descending passage very near to the subterranean pit. The ascending passage from the main entrance, it will be remembered, was found blocked up so that the entrance by this path into the corridor was "enjoined." Yet that glorious gallery with all its significant symbolisms might be gained through this narrow and difficult way up through the broken-out stone thirty-three inches from the gallery's north wall. Whatever this was intended to indicate, one thing is certain, that not through the Law nor through the Mosaic dispensation, its covenants or its circumcision, nor through the promises or privileges sealed to the Jews, could the gospel blessings be reached. God called that nation only to covenant engagements, and then sealed it. But by a new, a difficult, a narrow and yet a living way, through the death and resurrection of Jesus Christ, can the nations rise from the very borders of the pit into the glorious liberty of the sons of God, and be blessed with Abraham and his seed. Hence the wall of partition is shattered forever.

How could this be more clearly syllabled in monumental stone than it is here? The downward drift continues to the verge of the bottomless pit. The way into the grand gallery is wedged, sealed, blocked up. But a new, a difficult, narrow way leads to it through the chasm made by the burst-up ramp stone, symbol of Christ's atoning work.

This symbolism of the Pyramid was first suggested, not by the astronomer who visited the Pyramid for strictly scientific observation, but by a deeply pious converted Jew who had never been in Egypt. The account of this is given by the Astronomer Royal for Scotland:

"It was in 1865," says Prof. Smyth, "that a letter reached me at the Great Pyramid, transmitted with some high recommendations of its author, by that most upright knightly man, the late Mr. Maitland, Sheriff Clerk of the County of Edinburgh. 'He is a young ship-builder,' said he, 'a son of a ship-builder, an accomplished draughtsman, and I hear that he lately turned out, from his own design, one of the most perfect ships that ever left Leith Docks. From his boyhood upwards he has been an intense student of whatever could be procured concerning the Great Pyramid. His family surname is Menzies.'

"This Israelite, then, but no Jew, it was who first, to my knowledge, broke ground in the Messianic Symbolisms of the Great Pyramid, so intensified subsequently by Mr. Casey, and, after long feeling his way in an humble and prayerful spirit, at length unhesitatingly declared that the immense superiority in height of the Grand Gallery over every other passage in the Great Pyramid arose from its representing the Christian Dispensation.

"'From the north beginning of the grand gallery floor,' said Robert Menzies, 'there, in the southward precession, begin the years of the Savior's early life, expressed at the rate of a pyramid inch to a year. Three-and-thirty inch-years, therefore, bring us right over against the mouth of the well, the type of His death, and His glorious resurrection too; while the long, lofty grand gallery shows the dominating rule in the world of the blessed religion which He hath established thereby, over-spanned above by the thirty-six stones of His months of ministry on earth, and defined by the floor-length in inches (1881 inch years) as to exact periods. The Bible, fully studied, shows that He intended that first dispensation to last only for a time; a time, too, which may terminate very much sooner than most men expect, and shown by the southern wall impending.'

"Whereupon I went straight to the south wall of the grand gallery, and found that it was impending; by the quantity, too, if that interests any one, of about one degree (about six years); and where Mr. Menzies could have got that piece of information from I cannot imagine, for the *north* wall is not impending; he, too, was never at the Great Pyramid, and I have not seen the double circumstance chronicled elsewhere. The first ascending passage, moreover, he explained as representing the Mosaic dispensation. I measured it, and found it to be, from the north beginning of the grand gallery, the natal year of Christ, to its junction with the roof of the entrance-passage northward and below, or to some period in the life of Moses, 1,483 pyramid inches, and when produced across that passage, so as to touch its floor, 1,542 inches.

"But the chief line of human history with Robert Menzies was the floor of the entrance-passage. Beginning at its upper and northern end, it starts at the rate of a pyramid inch to a year, from the dispersion of mankind (2527 B. C.), or from the period when men declined any longer to live the patriarchal life of divine instruction, and insisted on going off with their own inventions, and which is sensibly represented to the very life or death in the long-continued descent of the entrance-passage of the Great Pyramid, more than 4000 inch-years long, until it ends in the Bottomless Pit, a chamber, already mentioned, deep in the rock. One escape, indeed, there was, in that long and mournful history of human decline, but for a few only, when the exodus took place in the ascending passage which leads on into the grand gallery, showing Hebraism ending in its original prophetic destination—Christianity. But another escape was also eventually provided, to prevent any one being necessarily lost in the bottomless pit; for, before reaching that dismal abyss, there is a possible entrance, though it may be by a strait and narrow way, to the one only gate of salvation through the death of Christ, *viz.:* the well representing His descent into *hades*, not the bottomless pit of idolaters and the wicked at the lowest point to which the entrance-passage subterraneously descends, but a natural grotto rather than artificial chamber, in the course of the well's further progress to the other place; while the stone which once covered that well's upper mouth is blown outwards into the grand gallery (and was once so thrown out with excessive force and is now annihilated) carrying part of the wall with it, and indicating how totally unable was the grave to hold Him beyond the appointed time.

" 'That sounds fair and looks promising enough, so far,' said Mr. Casey, 'but that is not enough yet to be the turning point with me, when interests so immense are at stake. We must have more than that, and something not less than proof of this order. Measuring along the passages backward from the north beginning of the grand gallery, you will find the exodus at either 1483 or 1542 B. C., and the dispersion of mankind in 2527 B. C. up at the beginning of the entrance-passage. Now you have already published, years ago, that you have computed the date of the building of the Great Pyramid by modern astronomy, based on the Pyramid's own star-pointing, and have found it at 2170 B. C. That date, according to this new theory, must be three or four hundred inches down inside the top or mouth of the entrance-passage. Is there any mark at that point? For I feel sure that the builder, if really inspired from on high, would have known how many years were to elapse between his great mechanical work in the beginning of the world and the one central act of creation in the birth of the Divine Son, and he would have marked it there as the most positive and invaluable proof.'

"So away I went," says the Astronomer Royal, "to my original notes to satisfy him, and beginning at the north end of the grand gallery counted and summed up the length of every stone backward all down the first ascending passage then across the entrance-passage and up the floor-plane towards its mouth, and soon saw that 2170 B. C. would fall very near a most singular portion of the passage. This was a line ruled on the stone from top to bottom of the passage wall, at right angles to the floor—such a line as might be ruled with a blunt steel instrument, but by a master hand for power and evenness. There was such a line on either wall, the west and the east, of the passage, and the two lines seemed to be pretty accurately opposite to each other. When Mr. Casey required, in 1872, to know exactly where, on the floor, the line on either side touched the plane, there was no ready prepared record to say. Every intervening measure by joints between the two extremes, and over scores of joints, had been procured, printed and published to the world in 1867; but just the last item required, merely the small distance from the nearest joint to the drawn line, was wanting.

"So I wrote to my friend Mr. Dixon, C. E., then erecting his brother's bridge over the Nile, near Cairo, requesting him to have the goodness to make and send me careful measures of the distance of the fine line on either passage wall at the Pyramid, from the nearest one of the two *quasi*-vertical joints, not giving him any idea what the measure was wanted for, but only asking him to be very precise, clear and accurate. And so he was, taking out also as companion and duplicate measurer his friend Dr. Grant, of Cairo; and their doubly attested figures were sent to me on diagrams, in a manner which left no room for misunderstanding. With this piece of difference measure I set to work again on my older joint measures of the whole distance, and was almost appalled when, on applying the above difference, the east side gave forth 2170.5 and the west side 2170.4 pyramid inches or years.

"'This testimony satisfies me and fills me with thankfulness and joy,' wrote Mr. Casey, while I never expected to have measured so closely as that along either side of those lengthy, dark and sloping Pyramid passages." *

In other words, it is found by the most careful scientific measurements that at 628 inches from the ascending passage, counting backward towards the entrance, are these two remarkable ruled lines. That ascending passage is 1542 inches long. Add this to the 628, and the date of the Pyramid is found. By the lettering on loose stones found by Col. Vyse this date was evidently 2170 years before Christ. By the astronomical calculations made at Col. Vyse's request by Sir John Herschel, this date was found to be 2170 years before Christ. And now, counting back from the beginning of the grand gallery 1542 inches, and then upward towards the main entrance 628 inches, the result is 2170 inches, where the two ruled lines are found—the symbols of erection, of building up and marking,—

---

* Smyth's "Our Inheritance in the Great Pyramid." pp. 430-437.

1. *The year the great Pyramid was built.*
2. *The advent of the God-man.*
3. *Messianic symbolism, an inch for a year in the grand gallery.*

The evidence is startling, that the builders of the Pyramid laid off those passages so that they should be historic scrolls of sacred history—an inch answering to a year. This confirms the conjecture that the ascending, blocked-up passage was meant to symbolize the time from the exodus to the birth of Christ—1542 years. Then it also follows that the Pyramid was a prophecy of the advent of the Redeemer, and a parable of the gospel dispensation. An inch for a year, counting backwards 2170 inches, marks the year the massive monument was built. 1542 inches mark the years of the Mosaic dispensation. And thirty-three inches from the beginning of the seven-fold gallery, mark the life and death of Jesus. Oh, it is wondrous! "*Mystery, all mystery,*" exclaimed the French savant.

"A sign and a witness unto the Lord in the midst of the land of Egypt."

Testifying to this infidel age the truth of God's word.

CHAPTER VII.

THE HISTORIC PARABLES AND PROPHECIES.

"EVERYTHING *is mysterious*," wrote the French *savant*.* "We are not at all enlightened, either upon the origin or the employment, the utility or any motive whatever for the grand gallery and its various passages."

Why those benches, or ramps, all along the sides of this long narrow passage, leaving a pathway of only two feet between them? Why these lateral slits or holes like little graves in each of those bench or ramp stones? Why these upright stones let into the wall behind them? Why the height of this passage 28 feet, while those leading to and from it are but four feet? Why those thirty-six great granite blocks spanning its narrow ceiling, and why its exquisite mechanical workmanship and polish? If it was intended for a passway only, why all this elaborate work and finish?

All indeed is *mystery*, only unfolded when the whole is viewed as a *parable in stone*—a monumental apocalypse of eternal truth and human history.

We have already seen how completely its

---

* Jomard, 1801.

mechanical data symbolize transactions the most important in their bearing on the world's destiny. These ramp holes or little graves, with the upright stones beside them, voice in impressional though silent eloquence, the resurrection from the grave following the resurrection of the Lord Jesus Christ. They commence, after the symbol of His resurrection; they succeed the uprooted ramp stone which is thirty-three inches from the beginning of the grand gallery.

And now, here is a remarkable fact in regard to those benches or ramp stones which border the corridor all the way up from the burst-out stone to the high step at its south end. The ramp stones are smooth and unmarked (except by the little graves already mentioned) for just four hundred inches from the beginning of the gallery; there commences a change. Along nearly the whole distance from 400 to 1800 inches of the western ramp, and occasionally along the eastern, there are longitudinal parallel scratches. " They are inflected upon and along its upper edge."*

Then further along from the beginning, from 640 to 1400 inches, these bench stones are fissured or parted from the walls, and *especially* from 1000 to 1317 the ramp stones have yielded, so as almost to break away the portion marked with the lateral holes or little graves.

---

* Smyth's " Life and Work."

Now as there is no pressure on these bench stones or ramps, which are, in fact, borders, (like our wash boards) all along the corridor—as they are seldom trodden on by explorers—the conclusion forces itself upon the mind that these fissures were formed in these stones when placed in position, and were designed as symbols of historic events connected with Christ's people. They must have been constructed as they now appear, and for what purpose but as symbols—*prophetic parables in stone ?*

Four hundred inches from the beginning of the gallery these scratches are "*inflected.*" In that year the general defection from the simple gospel began. Early in the year 400 A. D., Constantine the Great took the churches under imperial patronage, and pastors of independent churches soon began to aspire to princely rank. In the year 381, the second Council of Constantinople decreed that "the bishop of Constantinople should take rank after the bishop of Rome." A few years afterwards the Roman bishop claimed to be Peter's successor, and in 445 Valentinian issued a law "that the primacy of the apostolic seat having been established by the merit of the apostle Peter, the whole Church shall acknowledge the bishops of that city as rulers."*

Protests and separations from this law-church

---

* Neander, Vol. 11,. p. 174.

occurred all through the empire, followed by banishments and varied persecutions. A hierarchy was erected after the models of Judaism and Paganism. The *spiritual* true people of God, the true Church of Christ, fled into the wilderness. The heavy hand of despotic power crushed out their *visible* existence.

From the year 400 A. D. to the latter years of the 14th century, when Wyckliffe lifted his voice in England, and Huss in Bohemia, and the Waldenses in the Alps, the doctrines of the gospel, like the stone benches in the grand gallery, from the same and to the same number of inches, were marked, broken, "fissured," "and almost severed" from the foundation of the gospel.

In the Pyramid gallery the east ramp has yielded; from 640 inches to 1087 is frail material and "is fissured and parted from the walls, also the floor from the ramps."* Especially is this the case from 1087 to 1317. On the east side the ramp is broken away and the holes or little graves are almost entirely gone. The crumbling or decay of the stones here, both on the east and west side, surpasses any portion of the structure within or without.

At 640 inches, this "frail material fissured and parted from the walls" appears. In 622 Mohammedanism was established in the East, having

---

* "Life and Work at the Great Pyramid."

burst like a tornado from the desert. The transgressors had come to the full Maryology, and masses for the dead and priestly intercessions took the place of the worship and intercession of Jesus, the only Lord and priest. The darkness of Egyptian night prevailed. And from the time of the first crusade, till the hour that Peter de Bruys was burnt at the stake, 1144 A. D.—agreeing with these fissured and loosened ramps—the gospel was silenced east and west, and the traces of the true churches are lost sight of in the darkness and confusion, and deep apostacy of the times. From 640 to 1400 inches, the floor is parted from the ramp stone. From the year 640 (the missing stone), to the Reformation—the time of the Lollards in England and Waldenses on the continent—scarce a voice was raised in testimony of Christ and His truth.

These striking symbols with all their speaking fitness and significance, when taken *alone* have no seeming importance. But associated with all the vivid emblems of that mysterious gallery, they proclaim the Pyramid's interior a *parable of prophecy*, as the proportions of the exterior proclaim it a parable of scientific facts.

Passing up this wondrous chamber with its lofty ceiling spanned with thirty-six polished granite blocks which shelter and protect it—numbering the months of Christ's public ministry—with all its solemn, awe-inspiring mysteriousness—we come to a high step very near the gallery's close.

It is a part of the floor of the corridor, or grand gallery. It has the lateral holes or little graves cut in it, as the ramp stones have. Why this sudden step three feet high?

It is remarkable for being of softer limestone than any other part of the floor. It is cracked and worn, as is no other part of the *floor lines* in the Pyramid. The material of which this high step is composed was evidently selected for a purpose. The step itself is purposeless, and more than useless, except as a symbol. It is a sudden and unnecessary interruption in the ascent. If, as some suppose, the stone chest in the King's Chamber was brought up through this passage, or if anything else large, and heavy, and requiring care, was to be borne along into the inner chamber, this abrupt step of three feet would be an inconvenient obstruction. But there it is, and of frailer material than any other portion of the floor. It indicates a sudden uprise, associated with lack of stability.

This step three feet high occurs just 1813 inches from the beginning of the gallery. That number of inches corresponds with a remarkable year in elevated ranges of gospel service. It was the year following the close of the war between the only two nations in which Christ's people were awake to the duty of sending the gospel to the nations—England and America. It was a time of temporary peace through Europe. It was soon followed by the fall of Napoleon, and a *general* peace through the earth. It was the year when the British Parliament lifted the oppressive hand of the East India Company from off the missionaries who sought to reside and to labor in India. Up to 1812, missionaries who might arrive in India intent on preaching the gospel were "at once expelled from the country." Judson and Rice, the first American missionaries to the East Indies, reached that land of pagan darkness in 1812. While at Calcutta they were harassed by the East India (British) officials, and ordered out of the country, and had to retire to the Isle of France.

The great Wilberforce, after a twenty years' struggle, having been defeated in his advocacy of the "Indian clauses" in 1793, rose in triumphant eloquence to plead the cause of the missionaries in 1813, and on the night of the 22d of June of that year the "clauses" were passed in the British House of Commons by a majority of 53, and became law in India. The missionaries returned to Burmah. The British flag was henceforth their protection. Wilberforce had declared "this East India subject is assuredly the greatest that ever interested the heart or engaged the efforts of man"—"the greatest of all causes, namely, of laying a ground for communication to our India fellow subjects of Christian light and moral improvement," and then wrote in his private diary, "I humbly hope that

God has great designs in view for the East, and that they will be executed by Great Britain."

This Act of the British Parliament was followed by a general awakening through England and America, in regard to sending the gospel to the nations. It was an epoch in the history of the gospel dispensation. The day had come when "many should run to and fro and knowledge increase," and "this gospel of the kingdom be preached to all nations, and then shall the end come."

That year was followed by the advance in all that characterizes the activity and benevolence of the present age — discoveries, inventions, missionary organizations, public spirit and generous liberality in the founding and endowment of educational and humane institutions, the pride and boast of the hour. Society has been lifted to a higher plane, and Christianity in all its outward efforts and aggressive movements stands on a lofty step from which she can look back and down on the narrower and lower path trodden in past years.

But with all this intellectual and social progress, all this advance in the outward, the active and the material, where is the piety, the heart devotion, the calm thought and unshrinking faith, of these elevated and enlightened times?

As the high step in the Pyramid is of pliable or of less substantial material than any part of the floors either of the grand gallery or the other passages, so in all the boasted progress and advance of the present day there has been a crumbling away of basal truth. Vital doctrines have been and are ignored and even denied with levity, and often with derision, by the accredited ministers of the churches of the Reformation. Downright infidels have poured from Lutheran pulpits ridicule on the doctrines of grace preached by Luther. A bishop of the Anglican church is in foremost ranks of the impugners of God's word. Dignitaries in Scotland's free church have become the apologists and abettors of skepticism. In "evangelical" pulpits and theological schools of almost every denomination the *full* or *real* inspiration of God's word has been denied. *Work* is the watchword and *faith* is decried. The upward step is the image of that lack of rugged, steadfast, immovable faith which once distinguished the followers of the Lord.

The magnificent endowments of literary and theological schools, the erection of splendid houses of worship, the provisions made for the helpless, and the bond of sympathy established between distant peoples by which the public sentiment is aroused by the cry of the oppressed, and aid is rendered to the victims of flood or flame—all this is an upward step, elevating this nineteenth century above all ages of the past. Yet beneath all this is an emasculated, shattered, yielding theology, which places *humanity* above *dogma*—that is, a *depraved nature* above *divine truth, work* above *faith*, the material above he spiritual, and the present above the future. The time has come when "men will not endure sound doctrine." Well-paid musicians, and costly floral displays, and secular themes, and the sounds and sights in so-called evangelical churches, have taken the place of the glorious gospel of our blessed God. The upward step, fractured and marred as it was when placed there toward the close of the grand gallery, is a parable in stone of the days preceding Christ's coming. "As it was in the days of Noah, so shall it be in the days of the Son of Man."

What is the record of the years in which we now live?

"This is a delicate, soft-stepping, silken-slippered age," says a Christian philosopher, "patronizing the finer feelings and a high-flown emotional virtue; vice has cast away its coarse and tattered garment, and, though finding no great difficulty in obtaining admittance into good society, must come with sleek visage, in a spruce, modern suit, glittering with what seems real gold; the religion that languishes in luxurious aspirings or dreams, is very widely approved of. But does not an elevated and insidious but fatal pride tend to pervade the moral atmosphere of the time? We will glow in lofty ardor over the pages of Fichte, Carlyle, Schiller or Gœthe, but it is a balmy and consoling air which breathes its mild adulation through our souls; for is it not our own nobleness which is so gratefully evoked? We will worship in the Temple of the

Universe, with a certain and proud homage, like that of the stars, and winds, and oceans; but our lordly knees must not be soiled by getting down into the dust. We will perform with Gœthe the great moral act of self-annihilation, and wrap ourselves, with much ado, in the three reverences; but it were strangely bigoted to weep like an old Puritan because we cannot leap from sin, our shadow. Christianity, we proclaim, is pervading the age more deeply than ever before; not now as a constraining and antiquated form, but as an essence and life; not, indeed, with remarkable definiteness, not troubling itself to answer such minor questions as whether Christ's history is an actual fact, or whether Paul was an inspired preacher or a moral genius troubled with whims, but with a grand expansiveness and philosophic tolerance sweet to remark, casting a respectful and even deferring glance toward its plebeian ancestor of Judea, in whose steps, however, an enlightened descendant cannot exactly walk." *

This is the upward step—the close of the gospel dispensation symbolized by that three-foot step of soft and unendurable material at the end of the grand gallery.

And over this step the end or south wall impends. This may be noticed by examining the engraving. It leans as though it might fall over

---

* Bayne's "Christian Life," p. 44.

that remarkable step. The close may come at any moment, but its coming is surely near.

1881.4 inches is the floor-length of this wonderful seven-fold corridor. This is the length, however, when the calculated measurement is continued up the inclined floor under the step to where it ends *evenly* with the end wall. But the step itself is 36 inches high and 61 inches along or towards the end wall; that is, 97 inches from the line where the step commences. This makes the grand gallery floor line measure—

To the step..	1813	inches.
To top of the step...............................	36	"
Along the step.....................................	61	"
Whole floor length.............................	1910	"

If these symbolisms are true, if there was an object in all this elaborate work in the grand gallery, if the 33 inches mark the period from Christ's birth to His death and resurrection—unless all these wondrous symbols are treated, as they will be by millions, as trifles deserving no attention—if there is any truth in God's Book and reliance on its prophetic teachings, and correspondence between the times in which we live and those announced by the Holy Spirit as preceding the coming of the Son of Man—then the close of this dispensation is near, and the change is even now taking place, and *the time is at hand*. The teachings of the Pyramid as a parable in stone, correspond with the teachings of Christ in the parable of the virgins, and of the tares and the wheat.

CHAPTER VIII.

ESCHATOLOGY—THE GREAT TRIBULATION.

PASSING from the long and lofty corridor over the high step there is a sudden change.
The passage is low and narrow, with no ascent, but a dead level. The passage which leads into the grand gallery is fifty-two inches in vertical height. It is with bent form that it is traversed. But the one leading from its lofty corridor is only forty-four inches—the lowest passage-way, except the so-called Well, in the whole Pyramid. The transition is impressive. The change is abrupt, oppressive, appalling. From the high step, from the lofty granite-spanned ceiling, here is a narrow, low tunnel in traversing which one must move with pain.

What a speaking parable of the tribulation which Christ predicts must follow the close of this dispensation! Foretelling the close of this gospel age or dispensation Jesus said: "This gospel of the kingdom shall be preached in all the world FOR A WITNESS, and then shall the end come."* And again "and the gospel must first be published to the nations."† Then follows the time of sorrow, of tribulation, of

---

* Matthew 24: 14.
† Mark 13: 10.

eclipse and decline. Now the brother shall betray the brother to death. "And yet ye shall be hated by all men for my name's sake, but he that shall endure to the end, the same shall be saved." "For in those days there shall be affliction such as was not from the beginning of the creation which God created unto this time, neither shall be. And except that the Lord had shortened those days no flesh should be saved, but for the elect's sake, whom He hath chosen, He hath shortened those days."* Speaking of this same time—the end of the gospel age—preceding the time when "many of those that sleep in the earth shall awake," the Holy Spirit says through Daniel: "And at that time shall Michael stand up, the great prince which standeth for the children of thy people: and there shall be a time of trouble, such as never was since there was a nation even to that same time: and at that time thy people shall be delivered, every one found written in the book." †

A time of trouble such as never was. And the passage following the high step and the end of the gallery is lower than any preceding pathway. It is lower than the downward one along which the Dragon star gleamed.

But though so low, so difficult, it is short. It is only fifty-three inches in length. "But for the

---

* Mark 13 : 19.

† Daniel 12 : 1.

elect's sake he hath shortened these days."*

"Now," saith the Lord Jesus, "learn a parable of the fig-tree, when her branch is yet tender and putteth forth leaves ye know the summer is nigh." This He said in regard to the literal predictions just quoted. "The gospel is to be preached *as a witness* to all nations and then shall the end (of this dispensation) come." The high step, the elevation and advancement, the activities and enlightenment, the organized efforts to send the gospel every where, aided often by men who deny the full inspiration of God's blessed word—all these, like the leaves on the fig-tree, are the signs of the coming hour —or time of tribulation. The parable of the Pyramid corresponds with the parable of the fig-tree.

Fifty-three inches lead to a comparatively high but small room known as the ante-chamber. It is so called because it is so near, and leads into the principal room, or King's Chamber. This ante-chamber is about twelve feet high, five and a half feet wide, and nine and a half feet long. Its sides are ornamented with what may be termed wainscotting, or *dado* cut in the stone walls. These walls are part of granite and part of limestone.

Passing along the narrow and low pathway from the high step this ante-room is entered,

---

* Mark 13 : 20.

but just at the entrance is a double block of granite crossing the whole chamber from east to west. It is set in hollows cut in the wall, and rests on a ledge made by these hollows. This block of granite crosses the entrance-way into the chamber twenty-one inches from the wall and doorway. It has been supposed to be a part of a system of sliding doors, and the grooves cut all round the room, with no stones set in them, have been supposed to have been cut for a similar purpose. Hence this double block was called by Professor Greaves, two hundred years ago, the "granite leaf"—the word *leaf* being borrowed from the old term used to denote a sliding door over the water-way of the lock or gate of an English canal. The unfamiliar term, however, is confusing. It is better to think of it simply as a double granite entrance block, for it never could have been intended, as it never could have been used, for a sliding door, or portcullis. It rests solid—not loose, as some who have written on the Pyramid have said—on ledges formed in the wall by the hollows cut above these ledges, though not built into or connected with the walls. The double block—that is, one stone upon another—is made to fit into these grooves or hollows nearly midway from the ceiling to the floor. This double block is 15 inches thick and 48 inches in breadth from the grooves on the east and west wall—the part of the chamber above the grooves and wainscot being broader by 17 inches than the part of the room where this double granite block crosses it like a frowning judgment bar.

And this block of hard granite set there in the firm grooves has to be met and "undergone" by all who pass into the royal chamber. The thought involuntarily starts in the soul of every serious person standing before it and passing under it: "Has not this a solemn meaning, and is not that solemn meaning the test, the trial, the judgment—the day of decision and of vengeance, the great and terrible day of the Lord, when He will sit as a refiner—when the heathen shall be given Him for an inheritance and the uttermost parts of the earth for a possession, and He shall break them with a rod of iron, and dash them in pieces like a potter's vessel?"[*]

On that frowning granite block, that impresses one with what must be the crushing effects of its fall on any one passing under—grinding to powder and breaking to pieces as a potter's vessel—there is a jutting protuberance or bulb at its top. It is called the *granite boss*. It is the shape of a half moon, and has been carefully formed by the workman's chisel. It is exactly *one pyramid inch thick* and *five pyramid inches broad*. These are the ground elements of measurement throughout the whole vast structure. It symbolizes, indeed, *rule, measure* and *weight*.

---

[*] Ps. 2: 8, 9.

This whole ante-chamber is fairly syllabled with symbols of earth-commensuration and density. In entering it, all are confronted by this granite moveless standard which crosses and bars up the chamber, and on which are stamped the units of measure, the inch and the cubit. It seems to voice with eternal emphasis the declaration, "Judgment also will I lay to the line, and righteousness to the plummet, and the hail shall sweep away the refuge of lies." *

Like so many other things in this mysterious structure, there is no possible use or object for this double granite block unless it be symbolical. That it was not intended for a *portcullis*, or sliding door, is evidenced by the fact that it rests in the solid wall in which the grooves are cut for it to fit and lodge. This part of the wall would have to be cut down to the floor before it could be slid down so as to form a door. But then, as it is twenty-one inches from the wall where the entrance is, it could be passed even if it touched the floor. It does not reach the ceiling now, and if it were let down to the floor it could easily be scaled. "I myself," says the Scottish Astronomer, "sat above that double granite block, on *a ladder, day after day, with lamps and measuring rods, but in respectful silence, and generally in absolute solitude, thinking over what it might mean.*" †

---

* Isa. 28 : 17.
† Smyth's "Inheritance," p. 175.

In wondrous harmony with all that precedes it, this frowning block of granite which bars a chamber in which are engraven, in imperishable granite, rules and measures affecting the whole building and relating to all nature, is the symbol of the great day of decision, when in righteousness " He will judge and make war."

Passing under this double granite block called the " granite leaf," the ante-room is entered. It is a relief. The bowed form erects itself. The air, too, is different. A ventilating tube, though somewhat closed up, enters this room from the far-off exterior, and produces a felt change in the condition of the atmosphere. It is a mysteriously-built room—partly of granite, and partly of limestone. The proportion of these materials to each other is most significant. It will be noticed in full farther along.

Passing from this ante-room we bow beneath the *five* pilasters, made by grooves in the south wall, through a still lower doorway, being only 42 inches in height and 41.4 in breadth. Then follows a horizontal passway, the height and breadth of the entrance or doorway, and 100.2 inches long. It is all of granite. It will be observed that the granite work commences in the ante-chamber, except the thirty-six roof stones that span the grand gallery. All else till this ante-room is reached is limestone or marble. But here, in the ante-room, commences the granite work, mingled with limestone. What this signifies will appear as we proceed. From the ante-room *all* is granite. The narrow, low pathway which leads from it into the grand gallery is (floor, sides and ceiling) all of this significant material. The ante-chamber is a relief from the low passage that leads to it. It is over twelve feet high. After passing under the frowning granite leaf, or double block which bars its entrance, there is the ease and freedom of this twelve-foot high room. It is like the respite for "a little season" from the "tribulation" which succeeds the close of this dispensation.

But now comes a low, narrow passage again. All however, is granite, and its way leads into the glorious chamber of fifties — the King's Chamber, with its symbolic sarcophagus or coffer. Into this we now enter, and to it turn our attention.

CHAPTER IX.

THE KING'S CHAMBER—THE STONE CHEST AND THE ARK OF THE COVENANT—THE JUBILEE YEAR—CHRIST'S COMING AND KINGDOM.

THIS inner chamber, according to all who have written about the Pyramid, however they may differ in regard to other theoretical points, is the sanctuary, the centre and object for which the whole gigantic work with all it wonders was erected.

It is, in round numbers, 34 feet long, 17 broad, and 19 high. It is constructed of polished red granite—floors, wall and ceiling being of the same material. The blocks of which it is built, one hundred in number, are squared with nicest accuracy. The joints are needle-proof, though cemented together with a substance of the finest and most adhesive quality. "No autocratic emperor of recent times could desire anything more solidly noble, and at the same time beautifully refined."

When first entered by the Arabs, in search of the hoarded wealth of buried kings, they gazed in awe-struck silence on its red walls, which like polished jewelry reflected the gleam of their torches. Their wild shouts of *Alla Acbar* ceased. Pausing a moment in seemingly bowed

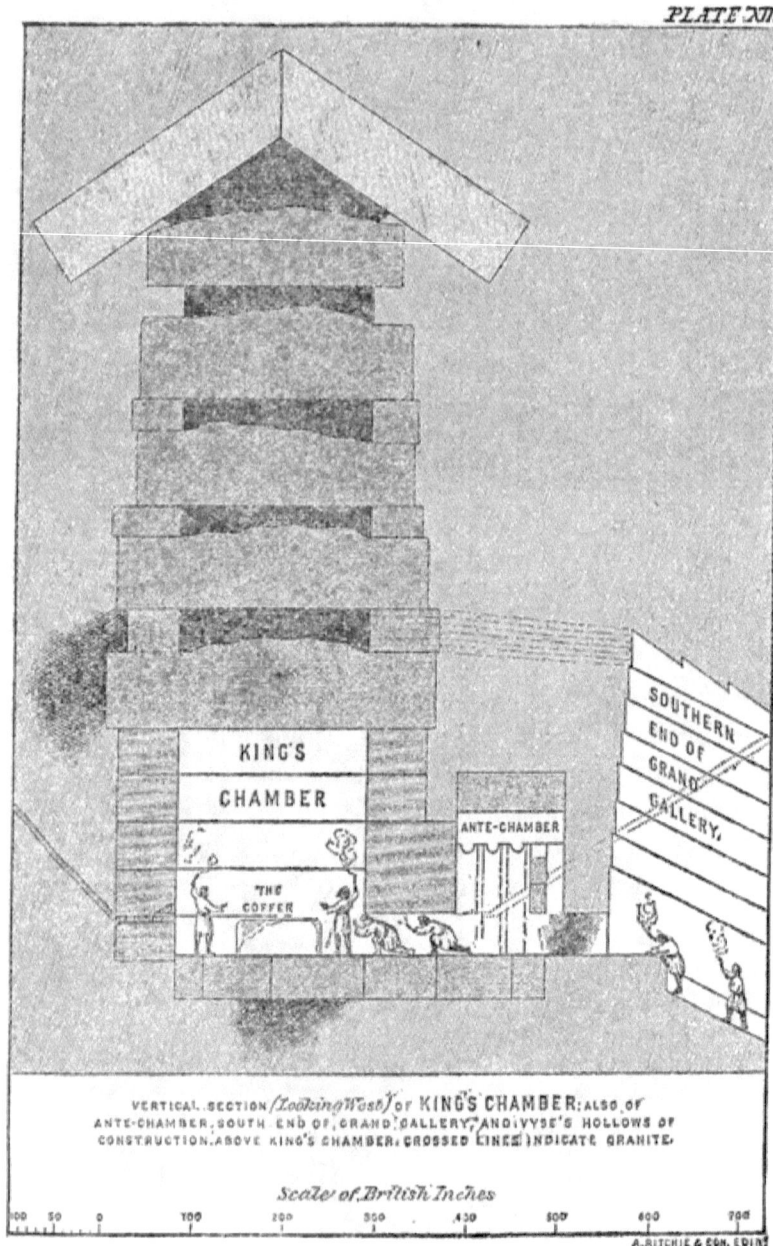

VERTICAL SECTION (Looking West) OF KING'S CHAMBER; ALSO OF ANTE-CHAMBER, SOUTH END OF GRAND GALLERY, AND VYSE'S HOLLOWS OF CONSTRUCTION ABOVE KING'S CHAMBER. CROSSED LINES INDICATE GRANITE.

Scale of British Inches

reverence, they looked noiselessly and cautiously for the priceless gems and charms which they expected to find treasured in this secret place. Nothing there, but a red granite stone chest, lidless, nameless and empty, while the pure unlettered polished ranks of red granite blocks, one hundred in number, looked calmly upon them from every side. Not a hieroglyphic (that is a priest writing) nor an idolatrous sign, nor a trace of anything Pharaonic or Egyptian, not a sign of kingly or priestly ambition or profanation there. Stainless as the cloudless skies above it, was that elaborately-wrought chamber. The red granite, empty, lidless chest, of exquisite finish, and which when struck rung like a bell, was the only furniture in the royal room for which the whole majestic pile was reared.

The same solemn, majestic and mysterious grandeur meets the eye and impresses the heart of those who enter that chamber to-day, except when thoughtless parties bent on hilarity, and exciting each other to levity, unite in their efforts to break the spell.

One of the first things to impress the serious visitor to this chamber, is the fact that it is built solely of granite. As before observed, all the rest of the structure, up to the ante-chamber (except the thirty-six stones that span the grand gallery) is of limestone. Those roof-stones of that corridor agree in number with the thirty-six months of Christ's public ministry. The double block set on ledges, and under which the visitor has to pass into the ante-room, is also of granite. It strikingly symbolizes Christ's judgments on the nations following the close of the gospel dispensation. Then commences a granite passage—a time of preparation, leading into this lofty royal room, which is all of polished granite.

If red granite—brought from a long distance, as none is found in Egypt,—was intended to symbolize the triumphs of the Redeemer, then here especially, at the close of all the passages leading to it, and in the chamber for which the whole structure was reared, red polished granite is the fit material to set forth and prove the latter-day glory, when He shall reign without a rival, and His people "shall be priests of God and of Christ, and shall reign with Him a thousand years." *

Next to this impression is that produced by the peculiar number everywhere marking this royal central chamber.

The walls are built in *five* horizontal courses, each course nearly four feet in thickness or height. These courses run all round the room, and the joints are so fine—indeed, microscopic—that the five layers or courses have been mistaken and described by writers for "*one* great slab reaching from floor to ceiling. * * * Noble

---

* Rev. 20: 6.

apartment cased with enormous slabs of granite twenty feet high." * But there are five courses of stone in the wall—not single slabs from floor to ceiling.

These five-times-five courses of stone are significant, especially if Chevalier Bunsen's interpretation of the word pyramid—*pyr-met*, division of five—is accepted. There is a niche, to which reference has already been made, in the chamber below this, called the Queen's Chamber, which has five ledges, or stories, its inner edge five times five inches from the center of the wall in which it is cut. In this upper royal chamber the *lowest* of the five courses of stone composing its walls goes down just *five* inches below the floor. This course is five inches less in height than those above it "by nearly one-tenth part, if measured from the base of its own granite component blocks which descend in the wall to beneath the floor's level." †

This *five* characteristic of the royal chamber is the more remarkable when it is remembered

---

* Lord Lindsey, 1837.

† Professor Smyth gives in full detail the measure of this room in his "Life and Work at the Great Pyramid," vol. 11. He accompanies these details with the measures of an engineer sent by a rich man to the Pyramid, with the object of "tripping up" the astronomer, if possible. The published results of the engineer's measurements completely confirmed Professor Smyth. See "Our Inheritance," p. 169.

that (as shown in the previous chapter) in passing through the lower doorway from the anteroom five pilaster-like marks, made by grooves cut in the wall above it, must be passed under to reach this granite room.

In addition to these five courses of stone forming the walls, the floor is on a level with the fiftieth course of masonry in the Pyramid.

There is something sublime in the contemplation of the masses of rock which form the step-like courses of the Pyramid itself. Standing midway up the mighty structure, as the writer has done, one feels that arrangements must have been made on a scale surpassing anything known on earth, and plans originating in the mighty minds were carried out with astonishing precision. Prominent among these executed plans is the level of this royal granite chamber with the fiftieth course of these vast layers of rock over the thirteen-acre base of the huge pile. And these courses, though different in thickness from each other, are each the same thickness all through every one course—that is, whatever height or thickness of stones any one course is begun with, it is kept on, at that thickness precisely, right through the whole Pyramid at that level, though the horizontal line may amount to whole acres.

"Having measured the thickness of every component course of the Pyramid one day in April, 1865, when ascending the summit, and another day when descending, I compared and confirmed these figures with my own photographs of the building, under a compound microscope, and also with similar numbers obtained from still more careful measures by the French Academicians in 1799, and then began to sum up the courses' successive thicknesses to give the whole height of any particular number of courses. On reaching in this manner the fiftieth course, lo! the total height of that stratum gave the hypsometrical * level of the floor of the King's Chamber as well as it has yet been ascertained by all the best authorities." †

The chamber below this, called the Queen's, is just twenty-five of these courses from the base, while this is fifty. It therefore may well be termed the Chamber of Fifties. Here, then, is a room with five and its multiples majestically engraved upon its shining granite. It has on its walls five courses of stone that seem like *one* It is placed on the fiftieth layer of rock in the Pyramid. It is formed of just one hundred stones, each of the same size, fives, ten times five, and twenty times five.

Fives mark the earth's polar diameter. It is five hundred millions of inches. Five marks the human form—the limbs parting with five extremities. Five senses mark the animal crea-

---

* Measure by barometer, boiling of water, or any other means than by triangulation.

† "Our Inheritance in the Great Pyramid," p. 173.

tion. The Hebrews were to march from Egypt in ranks of fives—a number hateful to the Egyptians. Five is the number of the Books of Moses, called the Law. Five times five is the ascertained length of the sacred cubit, the measuring rod of the ark and the tabernacles.

In the royal chamber stands the stone chest, the size internally of the chest or ark of the covenant. In that sacred chest were placed the tables of the Law, which Christ came to fulfill, the pot of manna, type of Christ, the bread of life, and Aaron's rod that budded, type of His resurrection. On that sacred chest or ark was the mercy seat, and the unfolding glory of the Shekinah. It was kept sacred in the *sanctum sanctorum*, in the secret place of the Tabernacle. It was preceded by the holy place, or ante-room. It was veiled and entered with bowed awe. It was made of *acacia*, and was itself lidless, though a mercy seat of pure gold was made to be placed over it. The chest itself was two and a half cubits long, one and a half cubits broad, and one and a half high. These measures, reduced by Sir Isaac Newton's valuation of the sacred cubit to pyramid inches, equal $62\frac{1}{2} \times 37\frac{1}{2} \times 37\frac{1}{2}$.

But this is outside measure, because height and not depth is spoken of, and especially as the mercy seat or lid of gold was to be made the *same* length and breadth; which, if inside measure, would make it fit into the box, or fall to the bottom, instead of being a lid resting even with its outsides. "If we consider the thickness of the sides and ends of the ark, 1¾ of an inch, and the bottom, 2 inches—a very fair proportion in carpentery for such a sized box in such a quality of (hard) wood—then its inside measures are $59 \times 34 \times 35\frac{1}{2} = 71,213$ as its cubical contents." *

Now, by repeated scientific admeasurements by Professor Greaves, the old Oxford professor, by Sir Howard Vyse, and especially by the Astronomer Royal for Scotland, with sliding iron measuring rods constructed for this very purpose—admeasurements, tested and compared by civil engineers, with all modern appliances—we obtain to the thousandth part of an inch the cubit capacity of the stone chest in the royal chamber—71,213 cubit inches. †

Here, then, with all the difficulties attending a true admeasurement to the least fraction, the wonderful fact appears that the sacred ark—type of the Redeemer—was the same size, in its internal capacity, as the stone chest or ark in the older and more gigantic work of man, this massive and mysterious pile. This stone chest, or ark, moreover, resembles a lidless coffin. So did the sacred ark, which God commanded Moses to make, with the same inner dimension,

---

* Piazzi Smyth's "Life and Work."

† For full statement of these measures and their confirmations, see Third Part.

and place in the secret and sacred chamber of the Tabernacle. Each resembles a coffin, or a tomb. For the empty, lidless tomb was the test and the glory of the Redeemer's person and work. The empty, lidless tomb is the token of triumph. God gave all men evidence that Christ's work was accepted, "in that He raised him from the dead."

"When first humanity, triumphant, passed
The crystal ports of light, and seized eternal youth."

The stone coffer in the royal granite room resembles a coffin or tomb. So did the wooden coffer in the holy of holies. But no form ever mouldered in that granite coffer. No one was ever buried there. Empty and lidless, it rested in its royal enclosure at the terminus of the varied passages through which it could not pass—passages whose measures all relate to this final one, and rise towards it with significant preparations and consummating beauty; the angle of ascent in those passages leading to it forming the radius of a circle equal to 36524+, and this again equal to the four sides of the base, and again, divided by one hundred, equal to the days, hours, minutes and seconds in our true year. Earth and heaven, all that concerns man temporally and eternally are symbolized, (whether it be by accident or design *) in this

---

* The temperature is 50; the mean density (of the coffer) of the Pyramid is 5.7, equal to the mean density of Earth's mass.

inner royal granite chamber with its symbolic tomb.

This symbolic tomb, this ark for whose lodgment this glorious granite chamber of fifties was constructed, has been proven by an eminent mathematician and investigator to be of the same dimensions as the brazen lavers in the Temple. Those lavers contained, from the Hebrew system of admeasurements, 40 *baths* or four *homers*. The Jewish *homer* has been shown to be equal to the Anglo-Saxon "quarter," still used in wheat measures. Four of these Hebrew homers or English quarters equal the contents of this "sacred" coffer. It is therefore the size internally of the brazen laver of the Temple. Those lavers are considered among all evangelical Christians symbols of "the washing of regeneration by the resurrection of Jesus Christ from the dead." Does the coffer in the Pyramid symbolize the same thing? Was such a glorious fact in God's dispensation of mercy worthy of being memorialized by the men who planned that vast pile and who expressed in its base and height, its location and position—the great facts in creation and the movements of the stars, which it has taken toiling centuries for scientists to reach?

But in the Temple, built to symbolize Immanuel, there was a vessel of still larger capacity than the brazen laver. It was the MOLTEN SEA. It was cast in bronze. Its cubical contents are given: "And he made a molten sea ten cubits from one beam to the other: it was round all about and its height was five cubits, and a line of thirty cubits did compass it about." "It contained two thousand baths."*

Now the brazen laver contained 40 baths: "Then he made ten lavers of brass; one laver contained forty baths," "and he put five on the right side of the house and five on the left side."†

So the Molten Sea was 50 times the laver—the 40×50=2000, the contents of the Molten Sea.‡

The cubic contents, or, in other words, the inner dimensions of the lower course of stones in this chamber, are just fifty times the dimensions of the stone chest. This layer of stones was sunk five inches below the granite floor, instead of resting on it, evidently for this very purpose. It is five inches less in height than the other courses forming the walls of the chamber. By the most pains-taking measurements, with the most ingenious scientific measuring-rods in the hands of experienced engineers, this result has come out. Then this lower course of stones composing the wall is the same dimensions as the Molten Sea in the Temple of Jerusalem, which is also fifty times

---

* 1 Kings, 7 : 23, 26.

† Verses 38-9.

‡ The Bath equaled 7 gallons, 4 pints, liquid measure, or 3 pecks and 3 pints dry measure.

the dimensions of the brazen laver, while the courses of stones which the floor of the chamber rests on is the fiftieth layer of rock in the Pyramid itself.

The Ark, the Brazen Laver, and the Molten Sea—expressive symbols of the redemption that is in Christ—seem duplicated in this chamber of fifties. It is the Jubilee number, and it is the Jubilee Chamber. The fiftieth year was the herald of deliverance and joy to the oppressed Jew. It was the acceptable year of the Lord—the type of deliverance from sin's sorrow and slavery.

It was the type of that deliverance for which "the whole creation travaileth in pain together" —the redemption of the body and the triumphant reign of the "second man, the Lord from heaven." The day is coming when the words of the angels will be fulfilled : "this same Jesus who is taken up from you into heaven shall so come in like manner as ye have seen Him go into heaven."*

It will be the realization of the vision of John: "And I saw a new heaven and a new earth," "the holy city, New Jerusalem, coming down from God out of heaven, prepared as a bride for her husband. And I heard a great voice out of heaven saying, Behold, the tabernacle of God is with men, and he will dwell with them, and

---

* Acts 1 : 11.

they shall be His people, and God himself shall be with them, and be their God."* "In that day the mountain of the Lord's house shall be established on the top of the mountains and exalted above the hills, and all nations shall flow unto it." † "The Lord God Almighty and the Lamb are the temple of it."‡ The Lord God and the Lamb will ever be the Temple, the light, the center and glory of that Tabernacle of God which will be with men. Surely nothing could have more fitly symbolized this glorious consummation of Christ's burial and triumph than the ark of acacia wood in the holy place of the temple; and surely nothing could be thought nearer in fitness to this than that ark of red granite in the inner sanctuary of this "oldest and most gigantic of all human works."

Over this chamber of fifties are those little rooms, to which access is found from the upper end of the grand gallery. There are *five* of them—of the same characteristics as the chamber below them, but unfinished, incomplete. May not those secret places, those little unfinished sanctuaries, typify the rest of the ransomed ones whom Christ will bring with Him at His glorious epiphany? "Those who sleep with Jesus will God bring with Him." Whatever these five chambers may mean, there is the

---

* Rev. 21 : 1-3.
† Isaiah 2 : 1.
‡ Rev. 21 : 22.

parable in all its fulness of the coming day of jubilee, when David's prayer shall be fulfilled: "And let the whole earth be filled with his glory. Amen and amen! The prayers of David, the son of Jesse, are *consummated* and ended."

CHAPTER X.

THE PYRAMID AND THE PLEIADES.

THE most popular living astronomer, R. A. Proctor, in an article in the *American Cyclopedia*, uses the following language :

"That the Pyramid was erected for astronomical purposes may be admitted; and we may accept Prof. Smyth's conclusion, 'that the building of the Pyramid corresponded to the time when the star *a Draconis* at its upper transit was visible (as well by day as by night) through the long inclined passage which forms one of the characteristic features of the Pyramid.' This would set the epoch about the year 2170 B. C. And it is a remarkable fact that, as Prof. Smyth points out, the Pleiades were at that time in a most peculiar position, well worthy of being monumentally commemorated; for they were actually at the commencing point of all right ascensions, or at the very beginning of running that great round of stellar chronological measuration which takes 25,827 years to return into itself again, and has been called elsewhere for reasons derived from other studies than anything hitherto connected with the Great Pyramid, the 'great year of the Pleiades.'"

The distinguished astronomer whose language

we have cited, accepts Professor Smyth's conclusion, "that the building of the Pyramid corresponded to the time when the star *a Draconis* at its upper transit was visible (as well by day as by night) through that long inclined passage which forms one of the characteristic features of the Pyramid."

We have previously dwelt on the symbolism of the Dragon star shining down that long passage to the subterranean chamber, or "bottomless pit." The astronomical fact is there—undeniable. But alongside of this is another fact equally patent. The tribes of earth, through all their history, have moved downwards in woe and crime to eternal darkness—have moved downwards under the malign light of some horrid principle of evil—some fatal spell—some monster spirit who has ruled in terror and in hate. "The world lieth in the wicked one," says God's Word. He is "the prince of the power of the air, the spirit that now worketh in the children of disobedience." He is called the "God of this world," "the dragon," "that old serpent the devil." To point to a north star might be a sufficient motive for building that long descending passage or excavating that bottomless, dark chamber. To symbolize the downward career of nations, the tragic and gloomy march of humanity, beneath the influence of Satan—this terrible fact of history was worthy of all the labor bestowed upon it. And there it is to-day symbolizing that melancholy fact.

But while *Alpha Draconis* looked down that dismal subterranean pit, the summit was lit by the light of the Pleiades—those gems of heaven whose beauty has fixed the admiring gaze of the pure and the thoughtful of every age.

The seven bright stars in the constellation *Taurus*, whose beams blend in soft splendor in our autumn and winter skies, are twice mentioned in God's Word, and man is asked, "Canst thou bind the sweet influences of the Pleiades?" Now astronomy has fairly demonstrated that there is a relative movement of all the star-galaxies round a central spot, and that this movement, like the march of mighty armies to celestial melody, includes every system in all the vast realms of boundless space. Sublime thought! Those still orbs, those countless throngs of trooping worlds—from the mightiest sun that lights up his circling system to the vidette star that looks out on infinite chaos—all move with a measured tread to an eternal time-beat round some central orb—the capital of the universe. The Pleiades have been shown, by the astronomer Medlar, to be that supernal center around which all these marshaled systems move—the great throne of the Eternal!

"Canst thou bind the sweet influences of the Pleiades?" as though God himself termed them the fountain of what men call gravitation—the source of all that binds the wheeling worlds in their orbits, as though this were God's palace, where He sits enthroned on the circle of the heavens.

The well-known "great year of the Pleiades" witnessed the completion of the Great Pyramid. The builders so planned and so labored that this "Pillar of Witness" should stand forth complete in all its grand proportions and all its wondrous symbols at the very time at which the Pleiades shone upon its summit—when its uplifted finger would point to the centre of the universe—to the throne of the Eternal. *

This movement of all the star-galaxies round one central point has been questioned. It would not be consistent with the design of this work to enter upon a discussion of theories on this or any other astronomical question. Kant first asserted the idea of a resemblance to our solar system in the movement of the stellar system.

---

* But by the retardation in the rising of the stars, already explained, or precessional cycle. it can easily be told when the Pleiades were on the meridian at midnight in Egypt. For we know that those softly-beaming gems of beauty now come to the meridian in latitude 30° the 17th of November—that is, 57 days after the autumnal equinox of 21st September. From the 21st to the 1st of October are nine days, which, added to the 31 days of October, make 40 days; and the other 17 of November make the 57. So that we know there has been a lapse of 57 days since the Pleiades were on the meridian of Egypt. Now as one year is to the lapse of this number of days, so is the precessional cycle to the lapse of years since the Pyramid was built.

"As the planets are kept at their proper distances and prevented from falling into each other, or into the sun, by the centrifugal force generated by their revolutions in their orbits, so Kant supposed the stars to be kept apart by a movement around some common center." "This theory of the stellar system, with some modifications, has been very generally held until the present time." *

It was objected that the stars remained *fixed* from generation to generation, and therefore could not be in motion round a common center. To this Kant replied that the time of revolution was so long and the motion so slow that it was not perceptible with our imperfect means of observation. The distinguished German astronomer who has confirmed the sublime theory of Kant, has also claimed the discovery of that center of the universe, and found it to be *Alcyone* (or *e Tauri*), the central star of the Pleiades.

But apart from this *seemingly* demonstrated fact that *Alcyone* in the Pleiades is the center, the Pretorium of the starry host, the other fact is unquestionable—that when the Pleiades crossed the meridian *above the pole* at midnight, 2170 years before Christ, *Alpha Draconis*, or the Dragon star, was crossing *below* the pole. It was in the autumn season of that one year when the meridian of the equinoxial point coincided with

---

* Newcomb's Astronomy, p. 471.

the Pleiades. It was, according to the usage of early times, the beginning of the year. It was, therefore, *the year* of the Pleiades, when they commenced that grand cycle which measures 25,827 years, that the Dragon star gleamed from below the pole down the descending passage of the Pyramid into the pit; while the central star of the Pleiades shone in soft splendor upon its lofty summit; the descending passage pointed to the Dragon; the summit, like an index finger, pointed to the center of the universe.

Monarch of all that human hands have reared, oldest and grandest thing that man has made, what are we to think of it?

> But thou, of Altars old or Temples new,
> Standest alone, none like to thee; for what could be
> Worthier of God, the holy and the true,
> Of human structures to His honor reared,
> Of a sublimer aspect! Majesty,
> Strength, wisdom, grandeur—all are aisled
> In this Eternal Ark of beauty undefiled.

CHAPTER XI.

THE CAP STONE AND CORNER STONE.

WE have gazed on the Pyramid in all its vastness, resting on its rocky bluff, on the borders of the desert, and looking over on the ancient land of Egypt—an altar to the Lord in the land of Egypt and a pillar thereof—a sign and a witness unto the Lord. We have entered its mysterious passages, and passed into its corridors, ante-rooms and royal chamber, tracing the symbols shaped in almost every stone. We return to the exterior. There it stands on a bed-rock whose depth has never been reached. What a type of the rock of ages, on which Christ's people are built? The foundation standeth sure, firm as the everlasting hills. On this firm foundation rests the imperishable building reared of massive stones. What a type of the building of God through the Spirit, of living stones, reared by His own hand and placed in the spiritual house by His mighty power!

The chief corner in this form of building is the *cap stone*, the head of the structure. In no other kind of building could the corner stone be the head, or cap stone. To this form of building with such cap stone, reference is evidently made in such portions of Scripture as "The stone which the builders refused is become the head of the corner."* The head stone of the lofty corner—or apex of the Great Pyramid, must be in shape a pyramid itself. The whole structure, too, must be built with a view to this corner. It may be said to have been built up into this corner stone, as God's people are said to be built up into Christ. It is different from any other stone in the building. These were square or cubical, or at least with rectangular corners. This single one had all its angles acute—all sharp points. It might well, therefore, be to the workmen a stone of stumbling. "Whoever fell on it should be broken" (or cut). "On whomsoever it fell, (from that immense height) it will grind them to powder." This top stone or cap stone, the head of the corner, could belong to a pyramid only.

This form of building, therefore, must have been before the mind of the inspired men who used this imagery to represent Christ. He is the foundation rock. He is the head of the corner. The crown and climax, the first and the last, the Alpha and Omega. "Jesus Christ being the chief corner stone; in whom the whole building fitly frame together groweth unto a holy temple in the Lord." †

---

* Ps. 118 : 22.
† Eph. 2 : 21.

The cap-stone is not now crowning that august edifice. And so Christ is not now the recognized Lord of earth. Satan is "the prince of this world—the spirit that now worketh in the children of disobedience." But

> " He whose car the winds are, and the clouds
> The dust that waits upon his sultry march,
> When sin hath moved Him and His wrath is hot,
> Shall visit earth in mercy—shall descend,
> Propitious in His chariot, paved with love,
> And what His wrath hath blasted and defaced
> For man's offense, shall with a smile repair."

FOR THE CAP-STONE SHALL BE BROUGHT FORTH WITH SHOUTINGS OF GRACE — GRACE UNTO IT.

"NOW 'TIS MINE."

" I asked of Time : ' To whom arose this high
Majestic pile, here mouldering in decay ?'
He answered not, but swifter sped his way,
With ceaseless pinions winnowing the sky.

To Fame I turned: " Speak thou, whose sons defy
The waste of years, and deathless works essay !"
She heaved a sigh, as one to grief a prey,
And silent, downward cast her mournful eye.

Onward I passed, but sad and thoughtful grown ;
When, stern in aspect, o'er the ruined shrine,
I saw Oblivion stalk from stone to stone.

' Dread Power ! " I cried, " tell me, whose vast design—"
He checked my further speech, in sullen tone :
" Whose once it was, I care not ; *now* 'tis mine."

PART III.

APPENDIX.

APPENDIX.

I.

MEASUREMENTS.

The base of the Pyramid covers............ 13½ square acres.
The length of a base side..............9131 Pyramid inches.
The vertical height is.........5813 Pyramid inches. (484) feet.
Solid contents of the Pyramid.................10,340,000 cubits.
The mouth of the entrance passage is, above the ground..50 feet.
Entrance east of the center....................................25 feet
Height of Doorway...................... ....47.24 inches.
Breadth   "   ....41.56 inches.
Dips at an angle of:.. 26° 28′
Subterranean Rock Chamber, below the center of the base...100 feet.
Subterranean Rock Chamber is.....................46 feet long.
    "   "   "   .... 28 feet broad.
Ascending passage leading from the entrance to the Grand Gallery, has its junction with the entrance passage at the distance from its mouth of about ....988 inches.
Height of passage...47.24 inches.
Breadth   "   ....41.56 inches.
Elevation   "   ....26 degrees.
Southward up the first ascending passage to the commencement of the Grand Gallery is..........1542.4 inches.
The floor length of Grand Gallery from north beginning to its southern terminus is...............1881.6 inches.
Height of Grand Gallery·...............................339.5 inches.

Height of the door at the north end of Grand Gallery is............53 inches.
Door at the south end leading to the ante-chamber............43½ inches.
From the beginning of the Grand Gallery floor to the well called *Souterrain*, is .... 33 inches.
The southern wall of the Grand Gallery impends 1 degree.
Length of Grand Gallery midway between floor and roof............1878.4 inches.
Number of roof stones to this gallery............36
" overlapping stones on side walls............7
Cubical contents of Grand Gallery............36,000,000 inches.
Strange exit from the upper corner of Grand Gallery, above floor............28 feet.
Length of short passage leading from the Grand Gallery to the ante-chamber is ....52.5 inches.
Length of ante-chamber............116.26 inches.
Breadth from east to west............65 inches.
The height............149 inches.
Thickness of Wall of passage-way between ante and King's Chamber............100 inches.
Length of King's Chamber............412 inches.
Breadth " " ....206 inches.
Height " " ....230 inches.
Masonry shielding King's Chamber from outside heat or cold............180 feet.
Temperature of King's Chamber............50 degrees.
Courses of masonry from base of Pyramid to King's Chamber............50
Wall courses of granite in King's Chamber............5
Height of first four courses............4 feet
Fifth and lower one sinks one-tenth below floor.
Outside length of Coffer in King's Chamber............90.01 in.
" depth " " " 41.27
" breadth " " " 38.65

II.

HAVE NOT THE MEASURES GIVEN IN THIS WORK BEEN CONTRADICTED?

THE question which we have placed as a caption to this article must be answered in the affirmative. But in thus answering it, another must be asked—What force is there in such contradictions?

The measures of Col. Howard Vyse were taken with a care and precision which could not fail to approximate exactness. He spent months of time and a moderate fortune in his investigations at the Pyramid. His measures in the main agreed with the old Oxford professor who carefully measured the passages and chambers of the Pyramid two hundred years before him. Vyse's measures agreed also, with few errors on one side or the other, with those of the French engineers who accompanied Napoleon into Egypt.

With these and other measures before his eyes, Piazzi Smyth, a practical astronomer, whose life had been spent in the observation of star transits, and in measuring lines and angles, spent four months in measuring and remeasuring these same basic and other lines and inner passages of the Pyramid. He had instruments made for this express purpose—iron rods which could be pushed through slides and measured with scarce a possibility of error. As an example of his usual method we give his measure of the inside of the coffer. It will be observed that he measured the width, first at the top, then a little lower, and so down to the bottom, so as to find the least deviation caused by any unevenness in the sides. So of the depth—measuring at different distances from the ends.

INSIDE DEPTH OF COFFER.

" The measure of this element is taken from the inside bottom of the coffer—which is apparently smooth and flat—up in the shortest line to the level of the original top surface of the north, the east, and the south sides; and of the west side also, *presumably*, before it was cut down to the level of the ledge which runs round the inner edges of the north, east, and south sides, and all across the west side's top.

Part of length where observations were taken.	Part of breadth where observations were taken.			
Inches south of inner N. end.	Near East side.	Near middle	Near West side.	Mean at each part of length.
0·6	34·30	34·28	34·26	34·28
3·0	34·44	34·36	34·35	34·38
5·0	34·42	34·41	34·28	34·37
10·0	34·40	34·38	34·28	34·35
24·0	34·36	34·38	34·26	34·33
Mean at each part of breadth	34·38	34·36	34·29	34·34

General mean or inside *depth* of coffer = 34·34 British inches.
= 34·31 Pyramid inches.

The following, from Smyth's "Life and Work at the Great Pyramid," shows the difficulties to be overcome in getting its accurate measures, and the *almost* absolute certainty of the results:

"This vessel, the sole contents of the dark King's Chamber, and termed, according to various writers, stone box, granite chest, lidless vessel, porphyry vase, black marble sarcophagus, and coffer—is composed, as to its material, of a darkish variety of red, and possibly syenitic, granite. And there is no difficulty in seeing this; for although the ancient polished sides have long since acquired a deep chocolate hue, there are such numerous chips effected on all the edges in recent years, that the component crystals, quartz, mica, and felspar, may be seen (by the light of a good candle) even brilliantly.

"The vessel is chipped around, or along, every line or edge of bottom, sides, and top; and at its south-east corner the extra accumulation of chippings extends to a breaking away of nearly half its height from the top downwards. It is, moreover, tilted up at its south end by a black jasper pebble, about 1·5 inch high (such pebbles are found abundantly on the desert hills outside and west of the Great Pyramid), recently pushed in underneath the south-east corner. The vessel is therefore in a state of strain, aggravated by the depth to which the vertical sides have been broken down as above; and great care must be taken in outside measures, not to be misled by the space between some parts of the bottom and the floor, itself also of polished red granite."

These measures, let it be observed, agree within a fraction with those taken by Col. Vyse in 1837, and by Professor Greaves two hundred years earlier, and have been confirmed by J. A. Grant, a resident of Cairo, and Mr. Waynman Dixon, a distinguished civil engineer.

Over against all this is the statement of Mr. McGarvey, a theological teacher in Lexington, Kentucky, who recently visited the Eastern Lands, and has published a very interesting book of his travels and studies called "Bible Lands."

He spent some two hours at the Pyramid viewing its exterior, ascending to its summit and examining its interior. A very brief time of course could be given to each part, and the examination must have been very superficial.

He had a "tape line" with him and measured as he hurried along. His account of this is interesting. He says of the entrance passage:

"Our only mode of descending would be to slide down and butt our brains out at the bottom, or to have a rope tied at the outside to which we could hold as we descended, but for the fact that notches have been chiseled in the floor at equal intervals to furnish a foot-rest. These were so rudely cut that our boots were continually slipping on them, and but for the help of the Arabs, whose bare feet seemed to stick to the stones as if they were glued to it, we should have at last drifted into the sliding method above mentioned. With two Arabs to help each of us, and one apiece to hold a candle before us, we managed to get along without breaks or bruises, but to take accurate measurements under these circumstances required some patience, and much straining of our muscles. (Very probable, although he says nothing about the strain on his tape-line!) Here I note the first serious inaccuracy of measurement given in the little book of Mr. Seiss' called a Miracle in Stone. He gives the length of this chamber (p. 84) as 1000 inches, which equals 83 feet 4 inches. I am certain it is several yards longer than this."

Now in the first place Mr. Seiss never made any measurements — never even visited the Pyramid, and is guilty of no "serious inaccuracy." He simply gives in round numbers the scientifically-ascertained measurements of Greaves, Jomard (the French *savant*,) Col. Vyse, Piazzi Smyth, the astronomer, and Petrie and Dixon, civil engineers. These men measured foot by foot, repeating in some instances the operation a number of times. And they all give nearly the same result—the average being 988 inches.

But Mr. McGarvey, with no engineering pretensions, for whose accuracy no man of sense would vouch, while straining his muscle and held up by Arabs, brought out a measure

SEVERAL YARDS greater than those pains-taking, scientific astronomers or engineers.

A difference in fractions of an inch, as occurs in the different scientific measurements, is accounted for by heat, pressure, and the possible slip of the carefully adjusted iron rod; but how shall we account for a difference of *several whole yards* in his, Mr. McGarvey's, great feat of measuring while held up by two Arabs, and in a painful strain of his muscles.

This writer also gives a further account of his entry into the King's Chamber and his tape-line measures of the coffer.

"When we entered the King's Chamber, our *Arabs*, whose noise had been already very annoying, set up such a Babel of loud talking and quarreling with one another, that we could have no conversation. Every one wanted to magnify his own importance by telling what we already knew, and he was equally anxious to push his neighbor into the background so as to get all the *backshish* to himself. I finally succeeded, by yelling louder than all of them together, in bringing them to silence, and posting four of the candle-bearers near the four corners, while a fifth candle was held near us to throw a light on our measures (certainly very much needed). We first measured the coffer, or stone coffin, on the west end of the room, and the only movable object in the chamber. We found its measurement exactly [of course, and if so the only exact one ever made of it] 6 feet 6 inches in length,

2 feet 2½ inches in width, and 2 feet 8 inches in depth. These figures show that its interior cubit capacity is exactly 6,144 inches, whereas Mr. Seiss, in making it appear that its capacity is the same as that of the ark of the covenant made by Moses, represents it 9,250 inches."

We may repeat the remark that Mr. Seiss made no measures; he simply quoted those made by the practical engineers whose names we have given. But with these Mr. McGarvey, tape-line in hand, after some fifteen minutes in the chamber, amid the yelling of the Arabs, and with nothing but a candle "to throw light on his measures," joins issue. His tape-line measure under the candle-light, however hurriedly made, is *exact*. Theirs, though carefully repeated day after day, with sliders made for the purpose, and steel hoops to fasten them to the edge, counting to the hundredth of an inch—though tested two hundred years apart and re-tested by civil engineers again and again—cannot stand a moment before Mr. McGarvey's tape-line.

For instance, he says the depth is 2 feet 8 inches = 32 inches. Compare this with—

Professor Greaves	1638	34.3
Dr. Wilson	1805	34.5
Howard Vyse	1837	34.4
Piazzi Smyth	1867	34.34

This last measure was a three days' work, after the coffer had been swept out and then washed and sponged with soap and water. It was done with all the allowances for the loss of part of the west side of the original size—unknown to Mr. McGarvey with his tape-line and candle. It was done under the full blaze of light illuminating the coffer, with no one to disturb.

III.

LETTER FROM THE ASTRONOMER ROYAL FOR SCOTLAND.

15 Royal Terrace, Edinburgh,
May 4, 1882.

Dear Mrs. S. R. Ford:

Your very interesting letter of last month has just arrived, with your several Mms., including, not least, the grand testimonial to your worthy husband's Pyramid Lecture.

You ask me some crucial questions, but prefix them by far too high an estimate of the little I know and can say about the Great Pyramid; for I know only, as a practical measurer, certain facts of number, weight and measure; but the interpretation thereof may be destined to fall into far better hands.

These are no secrets, no mysteries; imperfections of mine unfortunately too many;—but within their limits of error, there are the *ipsissima verba* of the ancient architect, in the shape of the forms and sizes of the stones he was Diviñely inspired to introduce.

Now of those, and what he constructed with them, you desire to know about the grand gallery, so-called;—better as you call it the Gospel Gallery.

It is not a simple, unique length; there are

three lengths, as intended by the Inspired Architect, and made to be so by the manner in which he has introduced the great step, at the upper, or farther, or southern end of the gallery.

First, the shortest possible length for gallery is thus:

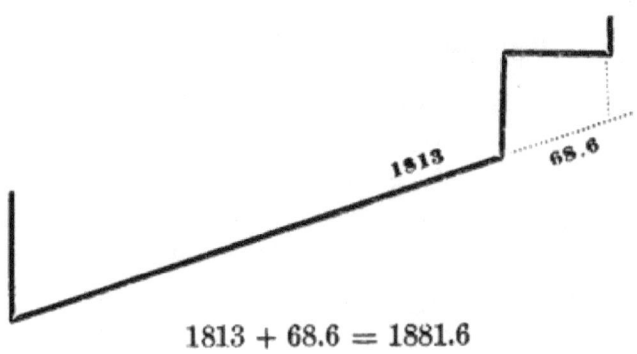

$1813 + 68.6 = 1881.6$

By measuring through the step in line of floor produced.

Second, the next shortest:

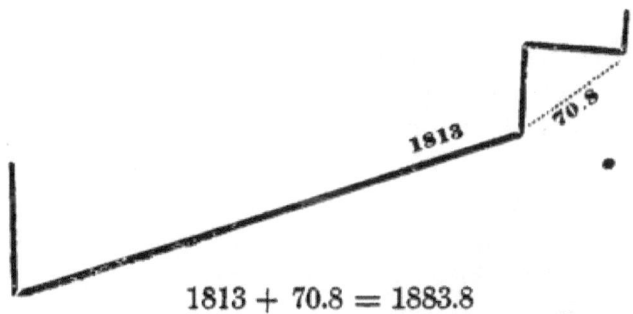

$1813 + 70.8 = 1883.8$

By measuring through step to corner of floor.

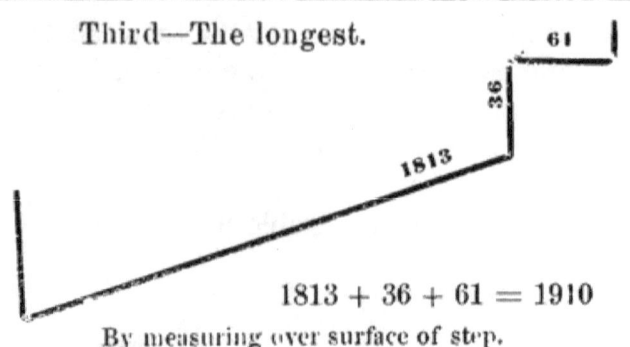

Third—The longest.

1813 + 36 + 61 = 1910

By measuring over surface of step.

Any one of these indicates that the time of the next great measurement of the Divine Ruler of the world and men is so near that we ought all to be never more watchful than now, for the rapture of the saint,—but need not expect the whole and final appearance of the Second Coming of Our Lord before all men, in power and in anger too, at this very instant. There is a little more time left still for repentance; but let no one presume how long; nor be disturbed at the events still to take place before that consummation arrives.

Meanwhile the dead-alive condition of Turkey, the persecutions and atrocities of Russians against God's people, the Jews, the rise of a new life in Egypt within the last few months, are all in the right direction, and bewilder the oldest diplomatic statesmen, who have gone on hitherto well enough, they think, without God in all their worldly calculations.

I remain, yours, respectfully,

C. Piazzi Smyth.

IV.

DID THE CAPHTORIM BUILD THE GREAT PYRAMID?

WHILE profane history gives no record of the origin of Egypt as a nation, the Bible sheds a gleam of light on its establishment, and points, as no tradition does, to the men who built the Great Pyramid.

Egypt is called to this day Mazr by the natives—a name most evidently derived from Mizraim, grandson of Noah. The fragments of Egyptian history which have come down to us, when stripped of fable, ascribe the establishment of its first monarchy to Mizraim in the year of the world 1816. Now we read (Gen. 10) that Mizraim was the son of Ham. "And Mizraim begat Pathrusim, from whom came Caphtorim;" and the very region in which the Great Pyramid stands was called Caphtor. Let this remarkable passage in Deut. 2:23 be noticed. God, encouraging Moses in view of the terrible enemies before him, tells him, "*The Caphtorim which came out of Caphtor destroyed them* (the Avim) *and dwelt in their stead.*" And in Amos 9:7, "Have I not brought up Israel out of the land of Egypt and the Philistines from Caphtor?"

The Philistines were Caphtorim. God did not permit them to be destroyed with the Canaanites. Caphtor was that part of Egypt where those Caphtorim lived.

This passing notice of the founders of prehistoric empires, shows that Mizraim founded the Egyptian monarchy; that his grandson, Caphtor, succeeded him, or at least held such position as to give name to the region where the Pyramid stands; and that his descendants were driven from Egypt. Their sojourn in Egypt is termed by Manetho an irruption. And Wilkinson (Vol. 1., p. 38) says: "From the preceding extracts of Manetho, as from other passages in his work, it appears reasonable to conclude that Egypt was, at one time, invaded and occupied by a powerful Asiatic people who held the country in subjection; and viceroys being appointed to govern it, these obtained the names of Pastors, or Shepherd Kings."

As it is now ascertained that the pyramids were built 2170 years before Christ, it is almost certain that these Shepherd Kings, or Caphtorim, built the Pyramids before the Pharaohs grasped the reins of government, and before the inhabitants became idolatrous and were brutalized by the most abominable superstitions. Herodotus was told by the priests that these men built the Pyramid, and that they went up to Canaan, and built the City of Jerusalem. How all this agrees with the reference to these Caphtorim!

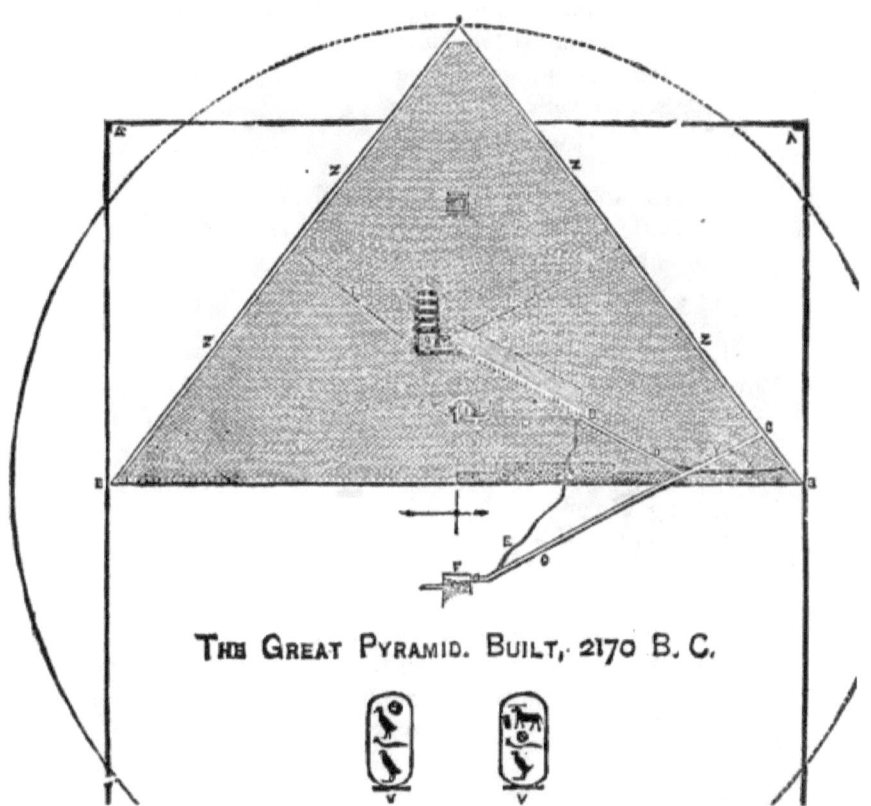

V.

INDICATIONS ON THE DIAGRAM.

A, A, A, A, Corner sockets of the Pyramid's base.
B, B, B, Pyramid cut in half, viewed from the east.
C, C, C, Entrance passage.
D, D, First ascending passage.
E, E, E, The well.
F, The subterranean chamber.
G, G, G, Native rock, left standing.
H, Horizontal passage to Queen's Chamber.
I, Sabbatic or Queen's Chamber.
J, Grand niche in Queen's Chamber.
K, K, Ventilating tubes to Queen's Chamber.
L, Grand Gallery.
M, M, M, Rampstones, incisions, and vertical settings along the sides of Grand Gallery's base.
N, Great step at south end of Grand Gallery.
O, Granite leaf in anteroom to King's Chamber.
P, P, Anteroom to King's Chamber.
Q, King's Chamber.
R, Grand Coffer in King's Chamber.
S, S, S, S, S, Chambers of construction.
T, T, Ventilating tubes to King's Chamber.
U, Supposed undiscovered Chamber.
V, V, Cartouches of the Kings, Shufu and Nem-Shufu, otherwise called Cheops or Suphis, and Sen-Suphis, or Noh-Suphis, under whose co-regency the Great Pyramid was built.
W, W, Sections of next two pyramids, showing their interior openings.
X, X, Al Mamoun's forced passage.
Y, Time-marks of the building of the pyramid.
Z, Z, Z, Z, Casing stones, now gone.

VI.

DR. PHILLIP SCHAFF'S OBJECTION.

IN his excellent book, "Travels in Egypt and the Holy Land," Dr. Phillip Schaff, after noticing very fairly Piazzi Smyth's measurements of the Great Pyramid and his deductions therefrom, asks, "If this was the design of the Pyramid, why is it not mentioned in the Bible?"

But it is mentioned by Job. And then the theory of Smyth is based on the fact that this mighty pillar is for a coming age—for the day when Egypt is "to cry unto the Lord." Schaff alludes to this wonderful prophecy in Isa. 19 : 19. "In that day shall there be an altar in the midst of the land of Egypt, and a pillar at the border thereof, and it shall be for a sign and for a witness unto the Lord in the land of Egypt." This, says Dr. Schaff, refers to a future event. Granted: but that future event is the witness it is to give—not its beginning or erection! This Pyramid has stood in its solemn grandeur through the ages—silent, objectless. It is now bearing record, as even skeptics and evolutionists are forced to admit. It does stand in the midst of the fan-shaped land of Egypt, and yet is on the border thereof. It is the only spot on which a pillar could stand and meet the demands of the passage—"in the midst of the land of Egypt and on the border thereof." So it is mentioned in the Bible.

But this learned writer asks, as others have, "Why all this symbolism confined to this one Pyramid?" But there is the fact—*it is confined to it.* There is no high science—no star pointing—no inner passages in any Pyramid but this. It stands alone in its marvelous disclosures, all the other pyramids being blundering imitations of this perfect Pyramid.

Why, then, it is again asked, was all this evidence of lofty intellect in those who built it—all this symbolism of the exact sciences, and of the dispensations of God, hidden so long from the knowledge of men—why left to this age to be uncovered and recognized?

The answer is on the surface. The Pyramid was reared in that early age as a memorial and a witness, which should disclose its long-hidden evidence in an age of scientific atheism and general apostasy. "*In* THAT DAY, it shall be for a sign and for a witness unto the Lord in the Land of Egypt, for they shall cry unto the Lord, and He shall send them a savior." Egypt is still under the heel of the oppressor; is still wrapped in darkness; she is not yet relieved from the curse pronounced upon her for her sins; she is still without God. But the oracle which pronounced her long night of oppression, also foretells her return to the Lord. And in that day shall this column of witness testify unto the Lord in the land of Egypt. Not till now have the wonders of the Pyramid been disclosed, and that disclosure is attracting the world, and scientific atheists stand dumb before its testimony for God.

Were the ruins of the Ark found amid the snows of Ararat, and measured and identified, it would be no greater proof of the origin of the race and the truth of the Bible, than is this voiceful monument " in the midst of the land of Egypt and on the border thereof."

Dr. Schaff, after describing with enthusiastic eloquence the view from the summit of the Great Pyramid, describes his descent and ascent through the inner openings or passages. "We came out covered with dust and perspiration, glad to reach the sunlight and open air."

As Dr. Schaff left them and hailed the sunlight and the breeze:—must he not have been struck with the thought, that the men who built this massive pillar had some object in constructing those recesses with such consummate skill and finish? What is that object? No meaning was ever depicted there—no idolatrous design mars their simple beauty. But their measurements and simple beauty *do* most accurately symbolize the event of the race—the revelation of the righteousness of faith through the atonement of Christ!

www.ingramcontent.com/pod-product-compliance
Lightning Source LLC
Chambersburg PA
CBHW032229230426
43666CB00033B/1648